Young Black Millionaire

How To Rise Above The Limitations Of Age, Colour And Race To Become Successful

Ezedi Souvenir Isaac

Email: youngblackmillionaire.mgt@gmail.com

Phone number: +2348142814580

Instagram: we_areybm

DEDICATION

This book is dedicated to my father, Mr. Solomon Azuka Alaba Ezedi, and to God Almighty for giving me the wisdom, courage, and strength to write it.

It is also dedicated to my idols, Vusi Thembekwayo and Steve Harvey, for unknowingly being part of my growth through their comical motivational videos and inspirational speeches.

CONTENTS

INTRODUCTION

Rising above the limitations of age, colour, gender, and race is extremely difficult, but if you follow the steps in this book, you'll learn how to rise above the limitations placed upon you by your gender, race, colour, age, or environment to become the great person you've always aspired to be.

The steps I scribbled down in this book are those I have personally tried myself as an African teenager and confirmed their effectiveness, as well as those I have studied in the lives of successful people who rose above certain limitations placed on them.

It was when I began to think in a totally different way and see things from an innovative perspective that I realised I was capable of much more than I thought I was. Let me start by saying that our minds were created to function extraordinarily, which is why the creator built them with the ability to stretch limitlessly.

A man once told me that the only thing limiting me was myself. I checked very well, and it was true. I rose from a broke African teenager living in Nigeria with no penny to his name to making a good sum of money online, and I've also seen people do it. You too can do it, and maybe even better. I have made this book clear, concise, and understandable even to the average person. This book comes with several quotes that I have written down at various stages of my life based on my observations, experiences, and inspirations. Use this book as a guide on your path to success.

WHO IS A YOUNG BLACK MILLIONAIRE?

To become a millionaire, you have to think, act and talk like a millionaire; then the millions will start coming in.– Ezedi Souvenir Isaac.

A young black millionaire is not necessarily a young, black, rich person. It is only an illustration I used to describe someone who has risen above the limitations of age, colour, race, and maybe gender to become successful. I don't believe that success is meant for a particular group of people; we were all built the same way, with the same brains and abilities, but along the way, some of us chose mediocrity, knowingly or unknowingly, because it's easier.

We were never created to be impeccable, but we were built with the ability to improve. The creator gave our minds the ability to stretch limitlessly so we could become phenomenal beings. It is also necessary to know that everyone of us has something that was given to us by God to make us stand out. Some of us just haven't discovered ours yet. Some have it but are still clueless on how to use it for their own benefits, while others intentionally keep theirs hidden.

I guarantee you that the journey to wealth and success is not an easy one, no matter the route you take. Even those who become successful through illegal means take lots of life-threatening risks. For example, the armed robber doesn't know the day he will be caught or the punishment that could be meted out to him. Success requires wisdom, courage, discipline, and persistence, but trust me when I say you can do it! It doesn't matter if you're American Indian, Asian, black, Hispanic or Latino, Native Hawaiian, or White. You just have to put your mind to it; after all, you weren't born for **mediocrity**.

WHY YOU MUST BE SUCCESSFUL

A man who believes in his heart that he will become successful, will keep trying no matter how many times he fails and how many years it takes.
– Ezedi Souvenir Isaac.

Everyone has their own definition of success. In simple terms, success means excelling at whatever you do, but I can proudly say that I measure success by the level of wealth one has accumulated. What good will a top football player's career be if he retires broke? Here are a few reasons why you must be successful:

1. Time isn't your friend; it's your servant.

Time is a bad friend but a loyal servant. You must be selfish with your time and utilise it very well in order to accomplish great things. Many people deceive themselves by thinking they have time when they don't, and no one does. If you want to live a better life in old age, start now and don't stop.

2. Death is coming.

Myles Munroe said in one of his books, "don't die old; die empty." Whether one likes and accepts it or not, death is coming, and there isn't one thing you can do to stop it. Most of us aren't conscious of the fact that we are getting closer to our graves as the day goes by. One thing you should never do is die with unachieved goals or unfinished tasks; die knowing you have done all the creator wanted you to do.

3. You will be a waste if you die unknown because the creator never built you to be mediocre.

Why be a pigeon if you were born to be an eagle? Don't crawl if you were created to soar. You've simply disappointed the creator if you die unknown with little or no accomplishments. The creator has great plans for us and has designed our minds with the ability to achieve great things, but only if we make the decision to do so. There's no difference between you and those great men. They just realised they were created for more and tirelessly worked towards achieving it.

4. You need to become successful because money influences everything important in your life.

Good health, good clothes, happiness, a proper diet, enjoyment, and even full service to God can be influenced by money. You cannot enjoy or live life to the fullest if you are broke. A lot of people have died from minor illnesses because of lack of money for proper medical treatment. Most of the necessary things can be bought with money.

5. Success attracts happiness.

Many people would say, "Wealth doesn't bring happiness." The right thing to say is that wealth doesn't guarantee happiness. There's a big difference between thinking about your problems on a beach in Hawaii or in the back of a Rolls Royce and thinking about your problems in your toilet.

I believe that even when you're successful but feeling down, if you take a moment to appreciate how far you've come and the things you've achieved, a unique form of happiness can emerge, unless you naturally tend to be ungrateful.

THE LIES

A lot of us are still facing financial problems in life because we have the wrong information about money. Any information ingested into your mind controls your action, and your action determines whether or not you'll be rich and successful. This is because the body is the servant of the mind, and if the mind is fed wrong information, it gives false or incorrect signals to the body. Below are some of the lies our society disguises as the truth.

1. Going to school will make you rich.

We often hear the misconception that going to school guarantees wealth, and that getting good grades is the key to success. In reality, having a university degree doesn't automatically make someone successful. Success depends on how effectively an individual uses the knowledge and resources at their disposal.

We are often admonished to go to school, get a job, start a family, and build a house before retirement, then retire and do nothing until death comes. I'm not against the idea of going to school, but I don't just want you to believe that it can make you rich.

2. Finding a nine-to-five job and diligently working is good for you.

If you pay close attention to the wealthiest men in the world, you'll realise that 95 percent of them aren't lawyers, doctors, teachers, or bankers. They're either entrepreneurs, musicians, movie actors, or athletes. Unless you're the CEO of a big company or the manager of a popular celebrity, the chances of you becoming rich from nine-to-five jobs are very slim.

One of the best career decisions to make is to become an entrepreneur. You get to make money and still be free. One disadvantage of nine-to-five is that it makes you not dream or have time to chase your pre-existing dreams. Here's my advice: if you are working nine-to-five, also work on your personal goals. Don't kill yourself for an organisation that would easily replace you if anything bad happened.

3. Savings can make you rich.

This is another lie we were told, especially as children. The only thing saving does for us is that it can save us on days when we experience financial challenges. People save so they can have extra funds for use when the need arises. Instead of saving all your money, take out sixty percent and find a business to invest it in.

We will talk about savings and investments later in this book.

4. Every rich person makes their money illegally.

It is really disheartening that some people still believe this, even in the twenty-first century. The poor feed their minds with this kind of information and develop a very poor and unhealthy mindset, which prevents them from making money or achieving financial freedom. Although some people acquire their wealth through illegitimate means but there are people who have true wealth that they have invested years of hard work and patience into.

5. Money can't buy happiness.

If money can't buy happiness, what can? Poverty? I've never seen a poor man who is truly happy because his financial status will always limit him. Money influences a large part of our lives, and there are things we can never have, places we can never go, and things we can never do if we are poor. The real truth is that money can make you happy but cannot sustain happiness because true happiness comes from within.

6. The rich are proud.

This is true for some rich people, but false for a lot of them. Most rich people aren't proud; they just don't want to mingle with ignorant and poor men who have nothing to offer. The proud ones are mostly those who were proud even as poor people. Money doesn't change a man; it only brings out the true character of a man that was previously concealed by poverty.

People become powerful based on the level of connection they have, which is why kings and lords in ancient times had lots of allies. I can guarantee you that if you can go to a rich man with something valuable to offer, he'll listen to you, respect you, and oftentimes, pay you. They value their time and won't give it away just like that unless you have proven to be someone important. So, before you expect someone with a net worth of ten million dollars to talk to you, ask yourself, "What am I offering him?"

7. Rich people are greedy.

The rich aren't greedy; they just don't settle for less when they could acquire more; they repel the ordinary and chase after the extraordinary. These people have come to understand that our creator built us to be exceptional, not mediocre. Therefore, it isn't greed. Greatness comes after one realises they were created to be more and to do more.

THE MOST UNACCEPTABLE LIE

This particular lie is one of the dumbest, though it is always told indirectly, especially by Christians. Some naive Christians believe rich people will never make heaven or enter the kingdom of God; this is quite humorous. Wealth can be a God-given gift, and he blesses men with it so they can bless their fellow men. Abraham, Isaac, and even Solomon were extremely wealthy, yet they were sincere servants of God. Wealth can only take you to hell if you acquire it illegally or refuse to bless others with it.

THE MOST ANNOYING LIE

The most annoying lie is that waking up early will make you successful. Many motivational speakers and podcasters often claim that waking up early is the key to success. As I was growing up, I read numerous books and listened to countless interviews and podcasts, where this idea was frequently promoted, even by individuals who were not verified millionaires themselves. However, the reality is that the time you wake up, whether it's 4 a.m., 8 a.m., or 10 a.m., doesn't have a direct impact on your financial success. Success is influenced by various factors, and early rising is not a one-size-fits-all solution.

Now imagine two men: one wakes up by 4 a.m. and the first thing he does is watch porn or scroll through social media, while the other wakes up by 9 a.m., starts by working out, and moves on to doing things that will change his financial situation. I believe the second man has a higher chance of attaining success. When we wake up does not matter; what actually matters is what we do with the day.

THE YOUNG BLACK MILLIONAIRE

Every one of us has something that was given to us by God to make us stand out. Some of us just haven't discovered ours yet – Ezedi Souvenir Isaac.

I watched as he stepped out of a black SUV car. Some security personnel clustered around him, and there was barely any way for people to get close to him. He was putting on a senatorial attire and a red cap. Some young men followed behind him, singing songs and praising his name.

An old man who stood in my corner shook his head pitifully at intervals. It was obvious that the man was either filled with hate, jealousy, or regret. "What did he have that attracted great respect from others that others didn't?" I asked myself. "Money!" I answered. I looked closely at the man and noticed he had almost the same features everyone else did. Same eyes, nose, ears, mouth, legs, and hands. He was black and lived in Africa, just like everyone else.

At the time, 90 percent of Nigerians complained of bad governance, yet he had so much to spend. I began to wonder how it is that some people have money in abundance and others don't. This prompted me to study the success secrets of wealthy people who rose above the limitations placed on them.

I began to read books, do research, study wealthy people, and try to incorporate their wealth-creation methods into my career and business. The more I worked, the more I was inspired to work. I had a strong belief that wealth wasn't meant for a particular group of people, and it pushed me to chase a better life. I wasn't willing to live a life of mediocrity and end up with regrets in my late years.

As I studied wealthy people, I penned down every experience with the hope of making it into a book later on. During the process of researching and implementing, I also learned my own priceless lessons, which I put down in this book. At every stage of my life, I was inspired to pen down certain quotes that can be helpful in making your life better.

I moved on to create a brand whose major aim was to provide financial literacy, business education, inspiration, and motivation, especially to those who believe that their financial challenges are a result of the odds against them. This brand is known as Young Black Millionaire Africa (YBMA). I believe in the existence of odds, but I also believe they can be used as ladders or stepping stones to greatness. Every problem comes to break you, but it is up to you to use your problems to your own advantage and make the most of them. I am Ezedi Souvenir Ifechukwude Isaac, and I'm the Young Black Millionaire.

CHANGE YOUR MINDSET, THE FIRST STEP TO SUCCESS

Two different entities live in us, both speaking at the same time but saying different things. The one that dominates is the one we listen to –
Ezedi Souvenir Isaac

Your mindset is a way of thinking, an attitude, or an opinion, especially a habitual one. It is a series of thoughts and beliefs you have about something. Having a positive mindset helps you see things for what they are and what they have the potential to become instead of what they are not; it opens your brain to see opportunities in every difficulty and make it a success.

Maintaining a negative and poor mindset is risky because your mind guides your body. If it's filled with negative information, it can send harmful signals to your body, hindering your progress.

WHY YOU SHOULD CHANGE YOUR MINDSET

1. It sets you up for success.

Until you change your mindset, the odds are that you will never be successful. You need to have a healthy, different, and positive mindset to attain success.

There's a saying that one's attitude has to change before one's altitude can change. You cannot prepare for success with a mindset that nurtures only failure. Your mindset can place you on the right track on your journey to success and keep you goal-oriented. Keep it healthy at all costs.

2. It changes your life positively.

When you start to see things differently, positive things begin to happen in your mind. Having a negative mindset is very dangerous because we often become what we think and talk about. A scholar taught that what we think produces energy in the universe and that if we think it often enough and long enough, it will actually produce a physical result in our lives. Your mindset affects your behaviour, and your behaviour affects your financial life. If you change your mindset, I guarantee that you'll begin to see positive changes in your life.

3. Changing your mindset can put you ahead of your peers.

Elon Musk is a billionaire today, and his childhood friends and bullies aren't because of his mindset. When you begin to think in a different and better manner, you begin to move ahead of your peers. I know this very well because I was very precocious as a young boy, and it placed me above my peers.

Most people would come to me for advice, and I always had something to offer; it was often helpful 95 percent of the time. Every great person you see today is where they are because they chose to think differently. It's hard to think differently, but to change your world, you have to change your thoughts.

4. It helps you relate with others.

One thing all successful individuals excel at is valuing relationships. You cannot climb the ladder of success alone; at some point in your life, you'll need help. That is why it is essential to have the right people around. Having a good mindset can help you attract better people and relate better with them, which can in turn be beneficial for your personal growth.

HOW TO CHANGE YOUR MINDSET FOR SUCCESS

1. Understand your current mindset.

Every inventor understood the old model of their products and how they worked before moving on to make them better. It is difficult to change what you do not understand. Assess your way of thinking and know the areas where negativity rules. In this way, you'll be able to change your thoughts and your perception of life.

2. Build Self-Confidence

Your success will be determined by your confidence and fortitude. If you develop self-confidence, you'll begin to see things from a different perspective, which will help in improving your mindset and developing your mentality. Self-confidence changes the way we see things and pushes us to achieve more.

3. Journal

Journaling is the art of writing down your thoughts, feelings, or emotions on a piece of paper. A journal is like a garbage can where you can empty the trash in your mind, like negativity, thereby enabling you to achieve a better mindset. The trick here is that when we write down how we feel, the things that happen to us, or what we want to do, we are able to constantly review and analyse them, know where we are lagging, where negativity or foolishness dominates, and know how to improve.

Get a journal and just write. Pour out your thoughts, feelings, and emotions. We will talk more about journals and journaling later in this book. It might seem a bit unusual, but I have a unique habit – I keep four different notebooks on my bed while I sleep. We will delve into the topic of journaling, and I'll explain this practice further.

4.Be optimistic

The best and easiest way to develop a healthy mindset is to practice optimism. Optimism is the act of seeing things from a positive perspective. The opposite of optimism is pessimism, which means seeing things from a negative, unhealthy, and detrimental perspective. I define optimism as seeing things for what they have the potential to become instead of what they aren't. There's a saying that an optimist sees opportunity in every difficulty, but a pessimist sees difficulty in every opportunity. One good way to become positive-minded is to appreciate the little things in life. You can only begin to get more when you become grateful for what you have.

5. Ask questions about things you don't understand.

I always tell people that wisdom begins with asking questions and extends to showing gratitude. We were never created to understand everything about life, but we were built with the ability to learn and improve. If you don't understand something, ask questions. It helps make you a better person. If you don't know how to ask questions, you'll give the wrong judgement to the right people and things.

6. Read often

This is my favourite method of achieving a good mindset. Every book you read is a reflection of the author's perspective, so when we read books, we begin to see things from other perceptions of life. This will be explained using what I call the stiff neck theory. An ignorant man is like a man with a stiff neck; he can only see what's in front of him, but when he begins to read and broaden his knowledge, his neck begins to turn, he starts to see things from other angles (perspectives), and his mindset begins to change.

7. Become a good listener

You can tell how someone feels by listening to them. I know it can be draining to listen to people at times, especially when their words are foolish. Becoming a good listener gives you an idea of how other people within or outside your circle feel about certain issues.

One thing that will help you develop good listening habits is knowing there is something to be learned from everyone, no matter how dumb they might be. Nigerian presidential candidate Peter Obi once said during an interview that he got advice from a mad man. It was quite funny, but I learned something from it.

8. Keep past events in the past and think about the future.

The major cause of an unhealthy mindset is negativity, and one of the causes of negativity is hurtful past events and experiences. Sometimes, our mind becomes like a garbage can because it is filled with our hurtful past experiences, such as heartbreaks, failures, and the loss of loved ones. If you must develop a better mindset, you must learn to keep the past in the past and chase after the future. The only thing about the past you should hold on to are the lessons and beautiful memories.

9. Believe that you can succeed.

Before taking action, I have a routine. I jot down what I intend to do, then I begin to picture it in my mind, visualizing every step towards success. Sometimes, I even imagine I'm in an interview, asking myself tough questions and practicing my responses. This process reinforces my belief that success is achievable, as long as you believe in it and work diligently towards your goals.

10. Speak positive things to yourself, especially in the morning.

Among the levels of creation are thoughts and speech. Speaking is the second level of creation. A scholar explained this with a theory called **group consciousness.** If one person keeps saying something long and loud enough, it will come to pass; if two or more people start saying the same thing, then it is assured that it will come to pass; and when a whole group of people start saying the same thing, it cannot help but come to pass.

Group consciousness is the name given to this theory. When you wake up, speak positive things to yourself and believe them, no matter your religion, and I can assure you, those things you constantly think and say will begin to transform into their physical equivalent.

11. Repel negativity

Another major source of negativity is naysayers, which is why you must carefully choose the people who are around you or who you want to be around. The people around you can greatly influence your life, either negatively or positively. If you surround yourself with positive-minded people, you cannot help but become positive-minded.

I've been in scenarios where I'm like, "I'm so confused and I don't know what to do," and my friends are like, "Calm down, it's going to be fine. We're going to figure something out." Automatically, I'm at ease because I trust my friends and what we can achieve together.

12. Move outside your comfort zone

There is a higher chance that you will not make it big or explore if you are still in your comfort zone. If you step out of your comfort zone, you will see life from a different perspective, which will help you develop your mindset. Some time ago, I visited an orphanage home in my hometown, and I can assure you that I became a better person after the visit. I began to practice gratitude.

13. Surround yourself with people who encourage and support you.

While I was in secondary school, my school always organised an inter-class debate competition, and often times, I was among those chosen to represent my class. At that time, I was in Senior Secondary School One (SSS1), and we were competing against our seniors in Senior Secondary School Two (SSS2).

When the competition began, my classmates cheered and supported me so well, yelling out loud. At first, I was scared and doubtful, but with the kind of support I got, I knew I had to win no matter what, and I did. The support I got helped change my mindset and build my confidence. No matter how hard you try to be different, the people around you will always have a great influence on your life.

14. Learn and practice the act of gratitude.

We lament so much about the misfortunes in our lives that we forget to celebrate the little wins. Instead of complaining, show gratitude for the little things you have and be confident that your sanity is assured. We only begin to get bigger things when we start becoming grateful for the little things.

The saying "as a man thinketh, so he is" underscores the pivotal role of our mindset in determining our achievements and character. If you harbour a negative or limiting mindset, your actions tend to align with those beliefs, hindering your progress. Conversely, a positive and growth-oriented mindset empowers you to take steps towards success. Often, people underestimate the profound impact of their thoughts, neglecting this vital element on their path to prosperity. In reality, nurturing a constructive mindset is akin to taking the first essential steps toward realizing one's ambitions and wealth-building goals.

It is very necessary for us to change the way we see things if we are to become rich. Our mind is a flexible mirror, and we must adjust it to see a better world. Once your mindset changes, everything on the outside will change along with it. A man once said, "to change your life, you have to change yourself, and to change yourself, you have to change your mindset." Some time ago, I read a touching story about a man who changed his life by changing his mindset.

During the first few years of a couple's marriage, they experienced difficult financial hardships, which dictated the state of their mindset. The husband had a start-up that was drowning, and they were struggling to make ends meet. They were in a very dark, deep financial hole and couldn't see any way out. The more they tried, the deeper they went. Then one day, the unthinkable happened: their electricity got turned off for non-payment.

After a series of unfortunate events, the husband screamed up to God and asked him, "is that all You had for us? Is that all that life has to offer?" Deep down inside, he knew the answer was no, and that was all the shimmer of hope he needed. From that day forward, he made up his mind that their light would never be turned off again, and he would do everything within his power to change all the financial problems they faced. And he did. It wasn't overnight, but he made up his mind that they wouldn't struggle anymore.

Until a financially broken man changes his mindset and perspective on things, there is a high chance that he will remain where he is. The young man in the story saw his problems as stepping stones to financial freedom instead of seeing them as the problems that they were, and instead of allowing their problems to pull them down, they saw them as a source of motivation.

There's also another story of a poor man who changed his mindset, thereby changing his life. This man lived in the same neighbourhood as a certain wealthy man who was an extravagant spender. Every day, he and his friends would criticise the wealthy man and accuse him of spending ill-gotten wealth.

To them, no one who made such money through legitimate means would throw it away like that. They kept hoping for his downfall, but instead the man became richer. One day, the foolish poor man decided to swallow his pride and ask the wealthy man two questions – how he made his money and why he was a reckless spender. He also asked him for help and the rich man replied, "I don't waste money; the parties you see me throw are fundraisers for different projects, and the expensive items I buy, I buy them as assets, hoping to sell them whenever their value increases."

The reason most people are still broke is because of mindset. They believe that most wealthy people get their wealth through illegal means, and consider all opportunities that come to them as scams without thorough research. Change the way you see things today, and you will be on your way to a financially free life.

ACTION STEPS TO TAKE

1. Try to find areas of your mind-set where stupidity, naivety, or negativity rules.

2. Work and commit to improving your mind-set and changing your perception of things.

FIND A SOURCE OF MOTIVATION OR INSPIRATION

Everything I see people do inspire me to do the same thing or something entirely different you – Ezedi Souvenir Isaac

A seven-year-old boy held his mother's arm tight as his tongue slowly caressed the ice cream she had bought him. They boarded a bike and hopped on as they were on their way back from the market, as that was the only mode of transportation available to them. During their journey, halfway to their destination, a sudden mishap unfolded. An oncoming bike lost control, leading to a collision that sent them tumbling. This unfortunate incident took place right in front of a petrol station.

In an unwavering display of maternal instinct, the mother instinctively shielded her young son from harm by using her own body as a protective barrier – a truly characteristic act of motherhood. Her efforts proved successful, as the boy emerged unscathed from the danger that loomed. However, the outcome was different for the mother, who bore the consequences of her selfless act. She endured, and continues to endure, a chronic knee injury as a result of her protective stance. This story holds a profound personal significance for me because, as fate would have it, I am the little boy at the heart of this narrative. This experience has become my most significant source of motivation.

To achieve financial success in a country like Africa, you need a powerful driving force. While the terms "motivation" and "inspiration" are sometimes used interchangeably, there exists a subtle but important distinction between them.

Motivation is the provision of an incentive or encouragement to someone to cause them to do something, while inspiration is the process that takes place when somebody sees or hears things that cause them to have exciting new ideas or make them want to create something. Motivation is like a propellant that pushes you forward. It's that internal or external drive that compels you to take action and work towards your goals. It could be the need to provide for your family, overcome challenges, or simply achieve personal ambitions.

On the other hand, inspiration serves as a spark that ignites your creativity and enthusiasm. It's often drawn from external sources, such as witnessing someone else's achievements or encountering a profound idea. Inspiration can kick-start your journey or help you see possibilities beyond your current circumstances.

Inspiration is also a person or thing that makes you want to be better or more successful. The incident with my mom was my biggest source of motivation, but my inspirations were different. There were people I looked at, and I was convinced that I wanted to be like them or be better; one of them was Vusi Thembekwayo.

My pastor joined the Navy because he saw a navy general, fully dressed in white, constantly appearing on television; that is **inspiration**. I became an entrepreneur because I wanted to make money and give myself and the people around me a better life; that is **motivation**.

One day, I went online and downloaded two photos, one of a Rolls Royce and the other of a roaring lion. I used the image of the lion as my home screen wallpaper and the picture of the car as my lock screen wallpaper. My friends and family saw a nice wallpaper, but it was a different thing to me. The Rolls Royce was to remind me that I needed to work because I hadn't driven the car yet, and the roaring lion was to remind me that I am an exceptional person who could do anything I put my mind to.

In my opinion, motivation is more important than inspiration. There are things you cannot achieve if you do not have a source of motivation. At times, the going becomes tough, and as a human, quitting becomes your easy way out, but motivation will keep you going. Why it is important to have an inspiration (a human) is for you to have someone you can copy their style of dressing, speaking, earning, or even general behaviour.

WHY YOU NEED TO STAY MOTIVATED

1. Having a source of motivation keeps you persistent while chasing your goals.

Every human being has that moment where they feel weak, tired, or experience imposter syndrome. During your growth journey, there will be times when you will have the feeling that you are not good enough, and quitting becomes the easy way out; but having a source of motivation will keep you on track. When I started my first blog, I didn't see any growth for the first five months.

At a time, I felt like stopping, but my motivation and desire to succeed were stronger than the challenges I faced at that time. Whenever you feel like quitting, picture that thing you really want in your head, and trust me, the desire to quit dies instantly and automatically.

2. Motivation boosts productivity and helps you achieve more.

Imagine you're a salesperson in an organisation, and your boss says, "I'll buy a Lamborghini for whoever can make one thousand sales in six months." Believe me, you'll access a different and phenomenal level of yourself. Most people would even go beyond the 1,000 sales. This is why the best workers in organisations are constantly rewarded or awarded.

The incentives given to them are meant to push them to work harder and encourage others to do the same. Your level of productivity increases when you have a source of motivation, and you'll be able to do and achieve more in a short period of time.

3. Motivation increases your intellectual capabilities and aids creativity.

All the engineers on Henry Ford's team who invented the V-8 engine needed to access a different version of themselves after a hard push from their boss. One day, Henry Ford came up with a crazy idea to create the V-8 engine. He pitched the idea to his team of engineers, and they said it was impossible, but to Ford, it wasn't.

He pushed them beyond their limits, and the impossible became possible. They achieved their goal and created the powerful V-8 motor engine. Ford motivated his men and made them utilise their intellectual powers and become more creative.

4. It improves focus.

When you have a strong source of motivation, you'll be more focused. You become more focused when your desire for success becomes stronger than the distractions around you. I was watching a free CSS course on YouTube with my PC one day, and suddenly, a notification popped up. It was quite tempting because it was related to the Transformers franchise, which produces some of my favourite movies.

Honestly, it took me a while to contemplate it, but I ignored it because my desire to be better at CSS was stronger and I wasn't the type to procrastinate. Having a source of motivation for whatever you do improves your ability to focus.

HOW TO STAY MOTIVATED

1. Look around you; what situations do you want to change that only money can?

There are situations that only money can change, no matter how much people try to twist them. There are ailments that you won't die of if you have enough money, one of them is HIV. If you do research, you will realise that most people who have died from HIV are poor or ignorant people. With antiretroviral drugs, an HIV patient can live a normal life, but the thing is, antiretroviral drugs don't come cheap.

Many challenging circumstances that people face are a direct consequence of poverty. Money, in many cases, serves as a potent solution to a significant portion of these problems. The question then arises: What are the situations in your life that you're fervently driven to change? These situations could manifest within your family dynamics, romantic relationships, friendships, or even on a broader societal scale.

Whenever you reflect on the fact that these situations remain unchanged, it often sparks a sudden, compelling urge to do more. This internal call to action becomes a powerful motivator, driving you to take steps toward positive transformation in the various aspects of your life and the society at large. The awareness of unaddressed issues becomes a catalyst for meaningful change.

2. Who do you want to prove wrong?

I had a lot of people I wanted to prove wrong; one of them was my mother, who believed that most rich people acquired their wealth illegally. I clearly understood her point of view, and I knew she was judging 100 percent based on the actions of forty percent. I was so desperate to debunk her statement. This was one of my sources of motivation. This can be a very powerful source of motivation; most people have achieved great things because they had people they wanted to prove wrong.

Enzo Ferrari, the founder of Ferrari, once said to a man, "You are a tractor driver, a farmer. You shouldn't complain about my cars because they are the best in the world." The man went on to create a supercar, which ended up being Ferrari's strongest competitor. His name was Feruccio Lamborghini.

Steve Harvey's teacher ridiculed him and said he'd never be on television. He strived to prove her wrong, and now he sends her a television every Christmas. You're free to feel hurt, offended, or angry about what people say to you, but use that anger as fuel to conquer them and prove them wrong.

3. Where do you want to be, and what are the things you want to own in the near future?

Constantly picture yourself in positions or places you want to be, and imagine yourself owning those things you've always wanted to. Knowing that there are things you want that you haven't gotten yet helps keep you motivated. Regularly think of that thing you want that you haven't gotten yet, and I can assure you, you'll hardly lose motivation.

4. Always endeavour to have those people around you who push you to become better, especially through their words of encouragement.

My biggest critic was my immediate elder sister, and she helped me improve in so many areas of my life. She also motivated me and pushed me to achieve more with her words. There are certain kinds of people you will have around you, and failure becomes difficult. Back then in secondary school, I used to participate in a lot of debate competitions, and my mom was extremely helpful.

There were times she would stay up all night listening to me, and she would never fail to point out places I faltered and encourage me to do my best. In whatever you do, surround yourself with people who encourage or push you to become better; it's healthy and necessary for your growth.

5. Look around you and find people you never want to be like, no matter what.

I have a weird habit of picking a book to read or researching whenever I hear someone say something extremely foolish. This is because I don't want to be or sound like them. One reason I committed to books is that I hate ignorance and mediocrity. Ignorance leads to mediocrity. There are people and events I see, and my desire to succeed becomes stronger.

My family house was close to the major road in my home town, and it gave us a lot of experiences. Some are fun, while others are hurtful. Sometime ago, I watched police officers harass a young man in my area. This man had no say and couldn't defend himself because he had no money and was also uneducated. He was struggling to speak.

From my point of view, the young man was right, but I'm not sure he knew he was, and even if he did, he couldn't do a damn thing to prove it. As a young boy, I decided that I'd never be broke or ignorant; this was another source of motivation.

FINDING A SOURCE OF INSPIRATION

One day, while scrolling through YouTube, I found a video, and to this day, I'm grateful I did. The video was an interview with Vusi Thembekwayo, a South African entrepreneur. I watched it and listened carefully, and I immediately admired the way he spoke, how intelligent he sounded, and his composure during speaking. At that time, I didn't know who he was, so I had to google him, and afterwards, I followed him on all social platforms. I was inspired just by watching him speak, and I wanted to be like him.

1. Analyse yourself and determine those people or things that push you to want to achieve more or become a better version of yourself.

This is the first way to find inspiration. To remain inspired, you must constantly watch and listen to these people who inspire you, also keep track of their lifestyles. I prefer human sources of inspiration to other sources because whenever I look at certain people, I become more inspired, and my desire to succeed becomes stronger.

2. Read successful people's stories.

This can be a source of motivation and inspiration. I find solitude in books, and one of my favourite genres of books is memoirs. Nonfiction beats fiction, no matter what. I like reading books about successful people, and I enjoy self-help books where the writer shares their personal experiences. There are things you read that inspire you, and you become inspired to do something phenomenal instantly.

3. Find things you want to change or improve.

Both innovators and inventors have something that inspires them to build their prototypes. For the innovators, it could be the former model of the product they intend to create or bad reviews about the previous version of the product.

For inventors, it could be watching people suffer from a problem. From watching or hearing people go through a particular challenge, a certain kind of inspiration springs up, and the desire to positively change or influence things comes up. Meditate, look around you, and ask yourself, "What do I want to change or influence?" and you'll be inspired to do something huge.

ACTION STEP TO TAKE

1. The only step available for you to take here is to find a source of motivation and keep it in your head. Remember it whenever you're feeling weak, tired, or unmotivated, and I promise you'll achieve more without realising it until the last minute.

FIND AN IDEA OR CREATE YOUR OWN PRODUCT

You're naive if you don't know what to do but you're foolish if you know what to do and you don't –Ezedi Souvenir Isaac

All you need to live like a king for the rest of your life is one good idea. Mark Zuckerberg designed so many things before creating Facebook. He doesn't have multiple businesses, yet he is one of the world's richest men. Facebook was all he needed to attain that. Bill Gates owns just Microsoft, yet he is a billionaire. You don't need multiple ideas to become rich; you just need one that is good and that you believe in.

According to the Oxford Dictionary, an idea is a thought or suggestion, especially about what to do in a particular situation. The idea I speak about is a special kind of thought put in the minds of men by their creator. You'll achieve more if you learn to work with your creator. Your creator speaks to you through your thoughts.

WHERE TO FIND AN IDEA

Your brain is home to multiple ideas, and with proper meditation and concentration, you will definitely extract one that will greatly benefit your life. In our minds, there are millions of thoughts; among these are those that can take us to the next phase of our lives.

HOW TO FIND AN IDEA

An idea is buried within the minds of every human on this planet; all we have to do is recognise it and then utilise it. You should find ways to do things that work for you and implement them. Approach problems with a strong desire to solve them, and ideas will come to you.

THE NEXT STEP AFTER THE GENERATION OF AN IDEA

Many people have died with a golden idea because they left it as an idea. Myles Munroe wrote something in one of his books, and I was deeply touched. He wrote that the cemetery is the wealthiest place in the world because it holds a lot of dreams and ideas. Don't be the guy who dies mediocre with unfinished goals, unimplemented ideas, and unfinished tasks.

The next thing you should do after successfully generating an idea is to write it down and work towards its implementation. You may think you have time because you are in your twenties or thirties. I want you to ask yourself an important question: "What is the probability that I'll live till the next week?" One truth most people refuse to accept is that our longevity is not assured. If you have an idea, don't leave it as an idea; work towards making it a reality, and in the end, you'll be happy you did.

Don't ever think any idea is crazy, dumb, or stupid. Often times, it is those ideas that are regarded as crazy that make the most money and become more successful.

WHAT IS A PRODUCT?

A product is anything that is grown or produced, usually for sale. A product can be manufactured or grown agriculturally.

HOW TO CREATE A PRODUCT

Find problems to solve and use novel ideas to create a product. There are lots of problems that are yet to be solved, and society will pay heavily for their solution. All you have to do is do your own research and find them out. These problems are grouped into two, which are:

1. Personal Problems

A lot of inventions and ideas have been brought to life as a result of particular hardships the inventor or implementer of the idea faced.

2. General problems

This is the second category of problems. Some inventions and ideas were also born because the inventor or innovator watched people suffer from a particular problem and sought a solution.

MARKETING A PRODUCT AND MAKING GOOD SALES

It doesn't just end at creating your product because, to make money, your product has to get to the final consumers who will pay you. One of the ways to make this possible is through marketing.

1. Be proud of what you do.

You become more driven to market your product when you love and are proud of what you do. There is a particular zeal that comes with being happy or passionate about a career, even if one has a low income. My very first step to effectively marketing a product is to be proud of what you do, believe in your product, and believe in yourself. Success might not come in the early stages, but if you're proud of what you do, the motivation will never die, and you will keep going no matter what.

2. Do a research on your product and the industry.

To become better than those who are better, you must research what makes them better. By researching the products that have been on the market before you, you learn how to conquer your target market.

i. Research rival products.

Before you begin the manufacturing or launch of your products, research rival products, learn about their strengths, weaknesses, and flaws, and build your product to be better. By doing this, you'll easily take control of the market in your early stages of operation.

ii. Research products with bad reviews.

Don't just research the good or seemingly perfect products; also research the flawed ones. The review section of every platform is a place to connect with the hearts of the people and know or understand what they truly want, how they want it, and where and when they want it.

Most times, the why isn't necessary as long as they pay you. Make research on those products labelled as bad or terrible by consumers and determine their faults. Use those faults to work on your product and make it better.

iii. Make inquiries about government policies related to your product or its industry.

There are products that have embargoes placed on them by certain governments, and there are companies dealing with unfavourable government policies. In order not to get stuck in the near future, do research and inquire about these policies and how to deal with them.

3. Know your target demographics.

Whether you're writing a book, releasing a song, creating a product, or bringing something new to life, ask yourself three important questions: Who are my customers? Who is my audience? Who needs my product? Knowing your target demographic helps you decide how to create your product to suit their tastes. I was to deliver a speech before some advanced people one day. The youngest among them were in their forties.

Knowing my audience helped me carefully select my words so I didn't sound strange or offensive. For example, if you are creating a product for children, you should add things that illuminate the product or make it fancier. Something they can relate to, so it intrigues or attracts them. This is why companies that produce school bags for children add pictures of superheroes or Disney characters. Know your audience, and then determine what they like.

4. Make your product beautiful

They say you shouldn't judge a book by its cover, but most people do, including myself. A book actually sold more than it ever has when the publisher changed the cover. A lot of people will buy a product just because of its packaging. Make your product beautiful and appealing to customers or consumers, and they'll buy it.

Some time ago, I wanted to purchase an energy drink in a store close to my area. I requested a particular brand I loved so much and always asked for, and while the woman was getting it from the shelf, I sighted another brand that was sitting on the shelf. The packaging looked colourful, and I hadn't seen it before. Immediately, I asked her to get it for me.

After tasting it, I realised it was better than the previous one. I gave the second product a try because of its look. I wouldn't have known how great it tasted if I hadn't given it a try as a result of the packaging. The same thing happens with humans; most people will favour you just because of the way you look. The prettiest girls get the nicest things.

5. Increase the quality of your product.

Don't pester people by telling them you built a house; build the house to a very high standard and let it speak for itself. High-quality products have the ability to market themselves. Imagine I had tried the second energy drink and realised it was terrible. I would have concluded that beauty misled me. It's not enough for a product to have beautiful and catchy packaging; it must also be effective. Your product must be able to do what it was created to do and do it well.

6. Increase the visibility of your product.

People can't buy what they can't see or what isn't available to them. Imagine that you produce liquid soap, and after production, you package it, store it in the warehouse, and leave it there with no distribution, marketing, or sales attempt. I'm very sure you won't make a sale. Every product you see sells because it was presented to people. As an entrepreneur or business manager, you must take advertising very seriously if your business is to grow and expand. Utilise social media as an advertising tool since it is easy to use and accessible to almost everyone.

7. Regularly keep track of your rival's product.

Business is just like war. During wars, both parties usually have moles in each other's groups whose main goal is to feed them information, enabling them to keep tabs on the actions of their opponent. To crush other products in your market or industry, you must regularly track their progress and know where they are improving or faltering, so you can make a better product from their flaws.

8. Create a website.

A website is a great way to take your business to the next level because it provides you with a space where your customers can come together and learn more about your products or services. You can add e-commerce features or completely make your website an e-commerce one, upload your products, connect it to a payment platform, and earn good money. Overall, having a website, especially one that is search engine optimised, helps you grow your business and sell more products.

9. Grow your email list.

I'm sure sixty to seventy percent of people have heard this saying: 'The money is on the list'. An email list is a list of the emails of your customers or potential customers. A lot of platforms grow their email list by allowing customers to sign up with their emails or incorporating a space for email collection. This is a great way to market your products. In your email newsletter, which you send to your customers, you can add deals, discounts, and products you intend to sell, which helps facilitate sales.

10. Regularly seek to improve your product.

Have you noticed how social media companies regularly update their platforms and add new features? This is because they are trying to maintain their relevance in the industry. If you don't do something to improve yourself or your product, you or your product will remain stagnant, and it is only a matter of time before you outlive your relevance or usefulness. A product is the best way to make money because you will be able to make money in your sleep. If you cannot create your own product, improve on existing ones.

ACTION STEPS TO TAKE

1. Sit in silence for a while and meditate. Try to find that novel idea or inspiration that you believe will change the world. No matter how foolish or crazy it looks,

Now that you've got your idea, write it down clearly on a piece of paper. Write a plan for your idea. Also, include the challenges you are likely to face along the way.

2. Challenge yourself to start taking small steps in order to make your idea a reality.

START SMALL

A valuable man doesn't seek opportunity; it finds him –Ezedi Souvenir Isaac

The journey of a thousand miles begins with a single step. The first step towards getting somewhere is to decide that you are not going to stay where you are. One major advantage of starting small or starting from where you are is that you get to make mistakes along the way and learn from them. Experience is the best teacher, and those who learn from it become outstanding students.

You should always know that time is not your friend, so you should learn how to make good use of it. A year from now, you may wish you had started today. John Dejoria is entirely self-made. He is most well known as the founder of the Paul Mitchell line of haircare. It would interest you to know that he started his career as a janitor and a truck driver. Then, in 1980, he formed John Paul Mitchell Systems with hairdresser Paul Mitchell with a loan of seven hundred dollars. He is now worth three billion dollars.

To become successful, start with the materials and resources available to you instead of yearning and wishing for things beyond your reach. If you want to be an entrepreneur, start with the little money you have and fund your big dreams later with the profits of your little business.

If you're a lawyer, no one says your first law firm has to be big, and if you're a writer, instead of sitting idle and waiting for big book deals, start out with the available publishing options you have. While you're doing this, always remember that there will always be room for growth.

There was a chain of petrol stations in the town where I lived, and they were owned by an individual—a woman, precisely. I was extremely curious about how a woman, especially an African living in such a remote area, could rise above the odds placed on her by gender and race to become a multimillionaire. I inquired more about her through my mother.

The woman started out as a roadside seller of petroleum products such as kerosene and fuel. She moved on to own about five petroleum stations in my town. This is one of the advantages of humble beginnings and small start-ups: you get to learn and grow over the years. This woman died as one of the richest people in my town, and everyone, both young and old, has not forgotten her name to date.

Another example is Sophia Amoruse, who started by rummaging through the racks of second-hand stores before moving on to begin her own fashion company, Nasty Girl. You must be able to access your current situation, determine the resources that are available to you, and determine the assets, resources, skills, or talent that you have to begin your success journey. You must begin immediately, without doubt, fear, or procrastination. The greatest people would not become so if they didn't have the courage to begin.

The best time to plant a tree was ten years ago, and the second best time is now. This is because time flies, and in the next ten years, you will wish you had planted today. Learn to recognise the little resources and opportunities in your life that can take you to the next phase of your life.

When I started my online money-making journey, I had a faulty phone with storage that was already full and no money to pay for a course, so I resorted to YouTube videos and doing research on Google. These were the only resources available to me at that time, and I utilised them effectively. I can proudly say I'm happy with the results I got.

BENEFITS OF SMALL START-UPS

Everyone wants to grow and become big, but the truth is that it doesn't always work like that. You learn, and you grow. It is the lessons you learn during your days of humble beginnings that will keep you going when you become big. Let's look at the benefits of starting from where you are.

1. Starting from where you are or starting small repels regret and sadness.

I stated earlier that, a year from now, you may wish you had started today. I also mentioned that the next best time to plant a tree is now. The feeling of regret is the source of depression in most adults. One major cause of regret is leaving things you were supposed to do undone, either out of fear, criticism from naysayers, procrastination, or discouragement.

Regret is a very dangerous thing because it is difficult to get over, and even after you do, the feelings come back occasionally and mess with your happiness. Start that business, write that book, record that song, and do that thing you always wanted to do before your bones become feeble.

2. Growth is guaranteed when you start small.

There is a tendency for most little things to grow. Every big thing you see was once small. If you start small, you will begin to make small mistakes and learn big lessons that will help you grow your business.

Most successful people we see today never went to the London Business Institute or any other business school to get a formal education, yet they do it so well. I asked myself what the secret was, and I figured it out after a while of deep thinking. I realised that all of these successful entrepreneurs, who had no formal education, had been in business for over ten years. The secret is experience.

3. Mistakes are less fatal at the beginning.

Starting a business with 1000 rands and then moving on to lose 500 is less painful than starting a business with a million rands and then moving on to lose 500,000 rands. Small beginnings repel big mistakes, which in turn helps you avoid a lifetime of regret. Sometimes, when you try to start from the top, you make fatal mistakes. It is very good to take risks, but it is much safer to take calculated risks. Everyone wants to become rich fast, and that's not a bad thing, but sometimes you may find it difficult to deal with the growth or make mistakes that will negatively and greatly impact your life.

4. Learning is assured.

Learning is assured when you start small. You can't skip learning during your growth process; the more you learn, the more you grow. I used to belong to an online community of blog owners, and one day a member asked the others to share their blogging experiences. Most of them confessed that they never learned about blogging or bought a course about blogging, yet they were successful and had even moved on to creating their own courses. They all learned from experience—making mistakes, failing, and learning. Starting small gives you enough time to learn and master your craft.

THE ULTIMATE TEACHER

There was a story my dad told me about my stepsister. When she was little, she always played around the stove, and at that time, they lived in London. My dad would always pull her away from the stove, but she kept going there. One day, my father was studying for his upcoming CT and guild exams, and my stepsister kept moving close to the fire. He made a very rational decision and ignored her while she went close to the stove.

Immediately, she cried out because she had just been burned. That was the last time she went close to fire. I will say this as loudly as I can: experience is the greatest teacher in life. Lessons learned from teachers or in school can never be compared to lessons learned from experience because experience sticks with you forever. You never forget them.

You have two choices if you must learn from experience: learn from your own experience or learn from other people's experience. This is why I would advise anyone who seeks success in Africa or any part of the world to get a mentor, one who will guide you based on his or her own experiences.

THE TRUTH ABOUT GROWTH

There is a truth most people don't know about growth, and they often make large mistakes because of it. Growth doesn't come quick, and when it does, you might not be able to handle it and then end up crashing. It takes years for a child who has just been born to get to 4 feet, not months, and if the child's body system begins to secrete a hormone called pitutarin excessively, he develops a condition called gigantism.

Growth should be one stage after the other; don't try to skip growth. Often times, people source large amounts of capital to start a business because they believe they will experience growth once this business has started running and be able to pay it back. I'm sad to say that it doesn't always work that way. I'm not trying to prevent you from dreaming big. Dream big, but start small and work your way up to achieving it. Quick growth is dangerous.

HOW TO START

The way to start is to just start. Start with you or your project looking ugly, rough, disorganised, or even lacking resources, but just start and make sure you never give up because there is always room for growth and improvement. Remember, everything that is small has the potential to grow.

PROCRASTINATION IS A DREAM KILLER

Many of us struggle to kick-start life-changing endeavours because we've fallen into the procrastination trap. For example, aspiring content creators might keep wishing to begin but they eventually delay because they believe they need better cameras. Likewise, someone with dreams of becoming an entrepreneur may hesitate to start because they think they require a substantial amount of capital.

What procrastination does is that it gives you reasons why you can't or shouldn't do what you need to. At the long run, it ends up killing your dreams and workforce. Procrastination often tricks your mind into believing that there will be a perfect time that doesn't exist. It makes you think you need substantial resources or the right connections before you can pursue your goals, leading you to delay taking action. In reality, waiting for the perfect conditions can hold you back from achieving what you want. Procrastination is dangerous because once you start, you can't stop it. It kills your productivity and your discipline. Get rid of procrastination immediately and start now.

WHY YOU SHOULD START SMALL

The benefits of starting small are quite different from the reasons why you should start small. Benefits refer to the advantages attached to small start-ups, and why you should start small refers to the reasons why you shouldn't procrastinate or relent and get doing.

1. Time isn't your friend.

There's this thing I hear a lot of people say: "I still have time." No, my dear brothers and sisters, you don't have time. This is one truth a lot of people hate to hear; you could die today, tomorrow, next month, or even next year. There is no assurance that one will live till old age, and even if you do, there'll be a time when your vibrant and energetic nature will be a thing of the past and all that will be left of you is grey hair, feeble bones, weak muscles, and maybe failing health.

This is the first reason why you should start. Time isn't your friend, but you're also lucky that it's your servant. One can either make their servant productive or not. What you do with your time is completely yours to decide, but please make sure it benefits you positively. Go out there and make a name for yourself, and try to achieve a lot while you are still in your prime so that even when you depart from this earth, your name and legacy will be implanted in the minds of every individual.

2. Starting small will increase your experience and make you an expert in your chosen field.

No one wants a mentor who has nothing to teach them. Men who have experience in any field are highly regarded and respected because of what they know. Starting small gives you the priceless gift of learning and growing, something you might not get anywhere else. When you grow in experience, you become more valuable and attract several opportunities for yourself.

3. You deserve all the best that life has to offer.

You deserve a good life, and you should start working towards it as soon as possible. I came home from school one day flaunting my termly result before my dad, expecting appraisals just like I got from my mom. My father took the results, took a closer look at them, and said, "You tried." Then he resumed studying his book.

I was surprised at his reaction and was forced to say, "Daddy, is that all you have to say? I am the fifth best in a class of forty." This means I'm ahead of 35 other human beings. He looked at me and said, "Someone took first, second, and even third, and they were all ahead of more people than you, including you. You deserve the best in life, and you should never settle for less, no matter how difficult life gets."

I learned a very valuable lesson that day. The superrich do not have two heads or two brains. There aren't demi-gods or some sort of supernatural being, so why should they live a comfortable and happy life and you an agony-filled one? This isn't an excuse for you to hate on them and hurt them; it's a call to do better. So get up and start; be persistent and resilient, and I can assure you that you will be sitting in the midst of those men and women you once worshipped in a short while. The sooner you start, the earlier you will get the life you desire.

ACTION STEPS TO TAKE

1. Write down all your big and small goals on a piece of paper.

2. Challenge yourself to start any of the small ones on your list and give them full attention. Once you become successful doing the small things, there is a tendency to be successful when doing the big things.

BUILD CONFIDENCE

None of us was created to be normal that is why the creator gave our minds the ability to stretch limitlessly – Ezedi Souvenir Isaac

Confidence is a feeling of certainty, firm trust, belief, or faith in something. The greatest quality a person can ever have is self-confidence. A man once said that the moment you doubt you can fly, you cease for ever to be able to do it. Confidence in oneself is very important. To succeed, you have to be confident in your abilities and trust yourself.

There is a story about two grains; they were lying side by side on a fertile soil. The first grain said, "I want to grow up! I want to put my roots deep into the ground and sprout from there. I dream of blossoming delicate buds and proclaiming the coming of spring. I want to feel the warm rays of the sun and dew drops on my petals." This grain grew up and became a beautiful flower.

The second said, "I'm afraid if I put my roots into the ground, I don't know what they will face there. If I grow tender stems, they can be damaged by the winds. If I grow flowers, they may be disrupted, so I'll rather wait for a safer time." So, the second grain waited until a chicken passed by and ate it.

Once we believe in ourselves, we can risk curiosity, wonder, spontaneous delight, or any experience that reveals the human spirit. As soon as you trust yourself, you will know how to live. I read a story about a man who bought a fake Rolex wrist watch. While some criticised him for living a fake life, I inquired why he did it. This man realised that to impress rich investors, he had to appear rich and confident. The Rolex wrist watch did a perfect job of giving him the confidence boost he needed.

It is easy to gain confidence; you must try to determine areas where you lack confidence and places where you experience imposter syndrome. Personally, one of the places I lacked confidence was in my writing; I always felt it was trash, even though the people around me thought otherwise. If you regularly speak good things to yourself, your mind and soul will believe and confirm them, which will give you a confidence boost.

Gratitude practice involves being grateful for the little things you have; this gives you the mindset that you can always get more, while overcoming fear and doubt simply means casting away every source of fear and doubt in you.

Self-confidence can help you in many ways, but most importantly in your journey to success. If you believe in yourself and in an idea, you would strive to bring it to life, and who knows? might hit your goldmine. Another important aspect of being confident is that people see you for who you are.

Imagine a sixteen-year-old boy walking into a room filled with successful men to make a business proposal, walking confidently, wearing a fine suit and wrist watch, and even speaking fluently. Then imagine another man, in his late forties, wearing a random cloth and walking shyly into the same room, maybe even speaking with his face down. Who do you think has a higher chance of getting the business deal? Of course, the teenager does.

WHY YOU SHOULD HAVE CONFIDENCE IN YOURSELF

1. Self-confidence helps you maximise your potential.

Fear and doubt are two things that kill potential in its birthing stage or at any level. You must develop confidence in yourself and be willing to try. Have the mind-set that you are a phenomenal person and that you can do anything you put your mind to.

2. It gives you the ability to start.

To start, you just have to take the first step. For instance, while I was writing this book, I documented a lot of lessons I learned, and my room was piled high with books, so I had to move some of the old notebooks to an empty room. I used this as an excuse to procrastinate and postpone the start of my book.

The truth was that I had never written a self-help book before and was doubting if I would be able to write it or not. I thought of hiring a ghost-writer, but they would never be able to do it like I wanted. After all, if you want something done right, do it yourself. I had to build up my self-confidence and tell myself, I need to try. Even if I fail, I'll keep learning and writing until I've gotten my book into bookstores. To be able to start, you have to build self-confidence, which will enable you to take the first steps. The good thing about starting is that you never know what's going to be big.

3. It is one of the qualities you will need to become successful, especially if the odds aren't in your favour.

If you're black or from an unfavourable race, young, poor, or have limited resources, then you must believe you will become successful before you become successful. Some of the people who accepted mediocrity did so because of the odds against them.

For example, someone took a cleaning job because it was the only job available to a person with no formal education. To make something happen, you have to believe you can make it happen. Let your faith in yourself and in whatever you are doing be stronger than criticism, mocking, and laughter from naysayers or from your enemies. Success begins in your mind, and it is then manifested into reality if you're smart enough, confident, hardworking, and persistent.

HOW TO GAIN CONFIDENCE

1. Workout or exercise.

One thing that has helped people gain confidence is exercise. Exercise gives you a better body shape than the previous one you had, and knowing you have a perfectly toned body helps build your confidence. This is why some women go through painful surgical procedures. We all want to have a nice body and be more confident in ourselves.

I was speaking with a friend one day, and we were discussing girls. He was like, "I'm a handsome guy with complete six abs; why do I have to go out of my way to get a girl's attention? While this might sound braggadocios, he's confident in his body because of his seemingly perfect appearance. Having a good body build helps you become more confident, irrespective of your gender.

2. Broaden your knowledge.

Humans become more confident when they know what to do or say in any situation. I'll explain this using a fictional story. Oak Street is an area that harbours all sorts of dangerous criminals; people who go to Oak Street are either robbed, raped, or killed.

Kennedy is a young man in his early thirties; he is tall, huge, and has a black belt in karate. Kennedy also moves around with an assault rifle. He decided to visit Oak Street, and his lady friend warned him of the dangers of Oak Street, but he moved on with his journey. Why? Kennedy is confident because he knows that if something goes wrong, he will be able to defend himself. There was a time when police officers didn't use guns, but the government began to issue firearms to them so they could be more confident in themselves while dealing with criminals.

There is this thing my mom used to tell us. She said, "If you see a ghost, just bend down, pack some sand, throw it at the ghost, and it will disappear." If you see a ghost, you're now more confident because you know what to do. The same goes for interviews and public speaking; you become confident when you know what to say. Read books, articles, or listen to and watch things that will help grow your knowledge.

3. Become eloquent.

Eloquence is another skill that gives you a confidence boost; being able to speak to people clearly also increases your confidence. Sometimes the way you talk or act while talking affects your confidence level. That's why public speakers are always advised to assume a particular position while speaking in order to gain confidence.

A lot of people don't contribute to public discussions and remain timid for the rest of their lives, not because they don't know what to say but because they don't know how to say it or express themselves. One of the reasons I adopted Vusi Thembekwayo as my role model is that he has the wisdom and the eloquence to give out the wisdom in a way that positively benefits the listener's life.

4. Positive affirmations.

What you hear either increases or decreases your courage and confidence. It doesn't matter if you hear it from people or from yourself. Even the Bible makes it known that faith comes through consistent hearing of the word of God. You have to learn to say positive things to yourself, even in negative situations.

There's this quote I use to motivate myself, and whenever I use it, I feel more energised to accomplish a task: "That which we are, we are – one equal temper of heroic hearts, made weak by time and fate but strong in our will, to strive to seek and not to yield." Speak positive things to yourself because when your mind ingests them, it boosts your confidence.

THE MAN IN A BOY'S BODY

He walked up to the podium as his shoulders moved in rhythm with his feet. He was dressed in a beautiful yet cheap suit, and on his feet was a black shoe. The investors were all seated, facing him, and eager to hear what he had to say.

"Good morning, everyone. My name is Joseph Martins," he said, beginning his speech. He was eloquent, maintained a good posture, had good negotiation technique, and was also very confident. One of the investors, a lady in her early fifties, suddenly had the irresistible urge to ask what his age was.

"I'm thirteen years old," he said with sincerity.

"Thirteen?" She asked with obvious shock in her face. "I'm still trying to remember what I was doing with my life at thirteen," she said as they all burst into laughter.

He's definitely a man in a boy's body," one of the investors said.

They all saw potential in the young boy, and instantly they knew he was destined for greatness, so they gave him a fair deal. He also got mentorship from some of the investors who couldn't offer him a deal.

PRIDE OR CONFIDENCE?

Pride and confidence are two things that are knowingly or unknowingly used interchangeably. The proud man thinks he's being confident, and people think the confident man is being proud. Confidence is good, but overconfidence is dangerous and is simply pride. Overconfidence is when you begin to think you can achieve everything all by yourself, even without the help of the creator. You must acknowledge the fact that you need people on your journey to success. Don't mind the motivational speakers, channels, or social media accounts that tell you that you become a dangerous person when you realise you can do it alone. You can't do it alone; you need help. You will die a death that your creator didn't approve of when you try to do everything alone.

The entrepreneur needs a customer; the music artist needs people to stream his/her songs; and a public speaker needs an audience. Be confident in yourself and your abilities, but honour all men and recognise how important they are.

Kill the boy in you and let a man be born—not just a man, but a great one.

ACTION STEPS TO TAKE

1. Recognise areas where you lack confidence. The first step in solving a problem is knowing the problem.

2. Make your own research and find ways to build your self-confidence in those areas.

3. Add workouts and studying to your daily routine.

4. Learn how to speak publicly and interact with people.

5. Use these two super-effective sentences and say them to yourself every day:

i. "I am a phenomenal being; I wasn't born for mediocrity, and I'll repel it at all costs."

ii. I can do anything I put my mind to, and nothing has the ability to stop me.

CONQUER FEAR AND DOUBT

The most beautiful things come from the toughest conditions – Ezedi Souvenir Isaac

Every human being was born with only two kinds of fear: fear of falling and fear of the dark. This means that your mind develops the rest as you grow older, and your mind can also conquer it. You can only move forward in life when you conquer your fears. You may be surprised to know that fear is a constraint on your progress.

Fear of trying, fear of starting, fear of asking, fear of rejection, fear of being mocked, fear of re-experiencing a past event, fear of poverty, and fear of death. All these are the common types of fear most people experience.

The Oxford dictionary defines fear as the bad feeling that you have when you are in danger, when something bad might happen, or when a particular thing frightens you. Fear has killed many dreams and ideas that were still in their birthing stages. Every successful person you see today had the courage to try, which is why they became successful at whatever they did. For instance, Mr. Beast, the famous

YouTuber, would never have found his goldmine in content creation if he hadn't tried it out.

Fear does so many things to the human mind. It makes you think you are not good enough and that your ideas and opinions are not good enough to be heard. It will keep you in the shadows of your peers forever, and you will remain in unseen shackles forever.

Yoda once said, "Fear is the path to the dark side. It leads to anger; anger leads to hate; hate leads to suffering." It is necessary to conquer your fear if you must move forward in life, because whoever is not conquering some fear has not learned the secret of life.

HOW TO CONQUER FEAR

1. Know your fears.

The first step in conquering an enemy is knowing the enemy, and the next is gathering as much information about your enemy as possible. You're in great danger if you have an enemy and don't know your enemy. To conquer your fear, you must first know what you are afraid of. Things become less frightening when you know all about them. I had a strict father who everyone in my family was afraid of. I was always the bridge that connected my father and my siblings; they would often plead with me to help them ask something of my father.

My sisters were scared of my father and didn't know how to ask, but I had studied him and knew effective methods to use whenever I needed something from him. If you know much about something, the fear you have for it will reduce or disappear completely. If an uncocked gun is placed on the table, an average person would be scared to touch it or even go close to it, but a person who has an idea of how guns work knows it is harmless until it is cocked.

2. Decide that you no longer want to be a slave to fear and man up.

Another way to conquer your fear is simply by deciding you don't want to be afraid again and speaking up. Decide that you want it more than you are afraid of it. Our minds are much more capable than we can imagine. If you make up your mind that the last thing that scared you will be the last, it will. There was a story of a girl who was physically abused by her stepfather and her mother. She lived in constant fear of her stepfather until she was seventeen. She decided she would never be scared of any man again, so she ran away from home and joined the Navy.

Everyone mocked her, and society condemned her. Esther trained until she became the best female naval officer of her time. You can use fear to your own advantage and as a stepping stone to greatness. You must understand that we cannot control what happens to us, but we can control how we respond to it.

It might interest you to know that I wrote the majority of my books during the period of eleven months that I was sick. I knew I wasn't going to die, but if I ever did, I wanted the whole world to read my book. See fear as a wake-up call for you to be braver, stronger, and greater.

DOUBT, FEAR'S TWIN BROTHER

I call doubt the twin brother of fear because doubt brings fear. When you're scared of doing something, you automatically doubt your ability to do it. Another parasite that kills dreams and ideas is doubt, especially self-doubt. In plain terms, doubt means disbelief in something and questioning that thing. It is very necessary to trust yourself and your personal capabilities because those who come through you today may not be there tomorrow. I always tell people that they are much more capable than they think they are; they only need something I call a trigger, and sometimes a hard one.

I had a neighbour who learned how to drive but was scared and doubted if she would ever get her wheels on the main road. Then, one night, her husband developed a very high fever. They were home alone with their two children, aged five and eight, at that time. It was late, and there was no one she could call or ask for help from. She had no choice but to drive him to the hospital herself if she ever wanted to see him alive, and she did. She would have continued to live in fear and doubt if her husband hadn't fallen ill. That was a hard trigger.

One effective way to conquer fear and doubt is to simply decide you want that thing more than you fear it or doubt you can ever get it. Let your desire for success be stronger than your fear and doubt. I remember how scared and doubtful I was the first time I wanted to pay an online influencer I'd never met before for an advertisement. I still went ahead with it because my desire to generate leads for my business was stronger than my fear and doubt.

Doubt makes you see yourself as weak and incapacitated; it gives you the mindset that you're not good enough; and it makes you believe that your golden idea will only remain an idea and cannot exist outside of your mind. This is why you must shun doubt and his twin brother, fear, in order to become successful.

Doubt can also come from the people around you, especially the simpletons and born naysayers. They will be like, "Bro, that's too big of a goal, and I doubt you'll be able to accomplish it." Don't forget to tell them to back off! And shock them with your success.

Another way to defeat doubt is to keep in mind that you are an exceptional and phenomenal person and that you can do whatever you put your mind to, no matter how difficult it may seem.

Types of fear you're likely to encounter on your growth journey and how to conquer them.

1. Fear of starting

This is the most dangerous type of fear, and it has killed so many dreams in its birthing stage. Sometimes we are scared to start because we do not know whether we will be successful or not. Life is a risk; everything we do is risky, so why not do the risky thing that could benefit our life? Conquer this particular type of fear by simply starting.

2. Fear of asking

I fall into the category of people who have this kind of fear. I'm the last guy who would ask you for help or a favour because I'm scared of rejection and negative responses. One day, I was scrolling through social media when I saw a post. It was a pictorial illustration, and in it, nineteen nos were in a sequence, and a yes was the twentieth and the last.

I pondered for a while, trying to understand what it meant. It simply means you can never get a no every time. There are eight billion people on planet Earth, and not everyone will hate you or be supportive of you. The simple way to overcome your fear of asking is to ask. Always be brave to ask; the worst that they could say is no, and don't stop when they say no. Make them regret it.

3. Fear of failing

There are times when we summon the courage to get up and start doing whatever we think is best for our lives, but we are often disturbed by thoughts of failure. Failure is not a bad thing because you are learning. Failure only becomes fatal when you don't learn from it. Have the mindset that even if failure is the worst thing that can happen to you, it can't stop you.

A man once said, "Remember, inaction breeds doubt and fear; action breeds confidence and courage. If you want to conquer your fear, do not sit at home and think about it. Go out and get busy. That man was Dale Carnegie.

4. Fear of being unable to handle growth.

This type of fear is uncommon, but there are still people who experience it. At a certain stage in your life, you might begin to develop thoughts like, "What if I cannot handle enormous growth?" and start feeling insecure. This is mostly common with entrepreneurs. Conquer this kind of fear by telling yourself that you can handle the growth no matter how big it is, and if you can't, you will get people to do it for you.

5. Fear of losing your assets or property.

The pain of working all your life for something and then losing it Either to divorce, accidents, or hoodlums. Do you know some super successful people are still single because they fear the concept of marriage and divorce? A lot of men have been reduced to nothing because of divorce. One way to conquer this kind of fear is to provide as much security for your assets or property as you can. It could be financial or physical security.

6. Fear of dying young or dying immediately after you encounter success.

This is another type of fear that almost everyone, rich and poor, encounters. Everyone wants to live long and enjoy life to the fullest. This is why rich people do everything they can to secure their health. Here are a few ways to conquer this sort of fear:

i. Prioritise your health.

Almost everyone has heard the common saying that health is wealth. You can achieve very little with failing health unless you're a very stubborn, resilient, or strong-willed person. When I say health, I don't just mean your physical health but also your mental health. There's still little you can achieve as a mad or depressed person. Here's what you should do: eat good foods with high nutritional values, workout, and avoid anything that affects your health negatively and decreases your chances of living a long life.

ii. Start early to work towards your goals, and don't stop or procrastinate.

If a child like Ryan Kaji can become a millionaire, then you're never too young to be successful. Don't mind simpletons. One reason why we have more male rich people than female rich people is that the men start on time to seek success while the women are still obsessed with K-dramas or Disney movies. Start early; the sooner you start, the sooner you can become successful and live a comfortable life.

iii. Seek your creator's or God's guidance and help.

Every man should walk in line with his creator if he desires a good and peaceful life. If you're a Christian, wake up every morning and pray to God. Be specific and tell him that death will never take you away when success starts coming or that you'll never cross over to the world beyond as a young person or a person with unachieved goals or unrealized dreams.

THE PHENOMENAL MAN

On a very special day, a being was born. People from every walk of life came to congratulate the being's mother, and there was joy all around. This amazing being was born, and the creator assigned a great deal of responsibility to him. The biggest is for him to never accept mediocrity. That amazing being is you. It doesn't matter who you are or where you come from; YOU WERE NEVER BORN TO BE MEDIOCRE. So conquer that fear and defeat that doubt. Go be and remain phenomenal.

ACTION STEPS TO TAKE

1. Make up your mind that you want to be stronger and braver.

2. The best way to conquer your fear is to do what you are afraid of doing. Gather as much information as possible about what scares you, then go ahead, do it and conquer it.

CHANGE YOUR DAILY ROUTINE

What you do every day either brings you closer to achieving your goals or pushes you away from your goals. – Ezedi Souvenir Isaac

What you do every morning somehow affects the rest of your day, whether positively or negatively. This is why Christians wake up every morning, and the first thing they do is commit their day to God and ask for his guidance, assistance, and protection.

I watched a video of a Navy general who said that if one wants to become successful, they should learn how to make their bed every morning. This is because making your bed is the first task of the day, and if you're able to accomplish it, it gives you a sense of pride and motivates you to get more done.

Juliana was a thirty-year-old, broke, and overweight lady, which repelled many men away from her. She was unbothered at first, hoping the right man who would love her for who she is would magically appear one day, just like in Disney movies. She waited until she was in her late thirties before depression eventually kicked in.

One day, she got a message from the dating site she was on: a guy had taken an interest in her and wanted to take her on a date. She was so happy; a man was liking her for the first time in a while.

The day for their date finally came, and Juliana wore her best dress and put on her makeup like she had never done before. She got to the venue for the date and waited, but Kelvin never showed up. She was frustrated and angry and about to go home when a woman in her early sixties walked up to her. The woman happened to be waiting for a friend who was stuck in traffic. She noticed Juliana's countenance and decided to keep her company.

Juliana and the woman started talking, and she opened up to her, telling her about her predicaments and how she was unlucky in love and broke at the same time. Her words were, "I feel the universe is against me, and I'm being punished for something I don't even know about."

The woman looked at her and said, "Have you tried doing anything to better your life? She began to lament all the things she had tried that were ineffective.

The woman smiled, looked at her again, and said, "What do you do when you wake up every morning?"

She replied, "When I wake up, I eat breakfast and maybe scroll through social media before preparing and going to work."

What kind of food do you eat, and what kind of work do you do? The woman asked again.

She disclosed that she was a fan of junk food and that she worked at a hotel as a receptionist.

Then the woman said to her, you are where you are because your daily routine never changes. You claim to be overweight, yet you don't work out, you still eat junk food, and you even do jobs that don't require you to move about. You claim to be broke, yet you wake up every morning and go to work in an office where you're underpaid. You don't think of or plan ways to change your financial status.

The problem is that men only want what's best for them, and honestly, you're not what's best for most men. Change your daily routine instead of lamenting about your problems, and see how your life changes."

The woman further advised her to reduce social media and replace it with reading, reduce junk foods and replace them with home-cooked meals, workout every morning instead of engaging in irrelevant activities, and find higher-paying jobs or start a business instead of complaining. Juliana realised the woman was right and decided to change her life by changing her daily routine, and in less than a year, her personal growth was noticeable to people around her.

Only a madman does the same thing and expects a different result. Ask yourself: What do I do every morning, and what do I need to change in my daily routine to be better? Every day, try to do something that will lead you to a better tomorrow. Aristotle said, we are what we repeatedly do.

HOW DOES YOUR DAILY ROUTINE AFFECT YOUR LIFE?

Have you wondered how people who master their crafts do it so well? You think it's just talent? No, it isn't. When you spend at least three hours every day trying to develop and master a skill, you will become unrecognisable in a year or less. The trick here is that when you do something productive every day, results are sure to come. It may not be too early or too quick, but I can assure you that it will come. The more productive things you do daily, the better your results will be. This is how your daily routine affects your life.

HOW TO CHANGE YOUR DAILY ROUTINE

A large part of your daily routine is dependent on what you intend to achieve. The bodybuilder wakes up and heads to the gym because he wants to stay fit; the stock investor wakes up and reads news about the stock market because he wants to stay rich and updated; and the pastor fasts because he wants his spiritual life to grow. I'm not going to write a step-by-step guide on how to change your daily routine, but I will help you do it yourself.

Look at yourself and ask yourself a simple question: where do I want to be, and what are the things I need to do to get there? When you answer this question, you'll realise what you need to do daily to be where you want to be. For example, if you want to be fit, incorporate exercise into your daily routine, and if you want to be smarter, incorporate studying into your daily routine. Overall, do at least one fun or refreshing thing and three productive things every day.

CONSISTENCY, NOT INTENSITY

I started writing as early as eight, but I wasn't very good, and I wasn't as good as I wanted to be even at twelve and thirteen years old. In a bid to be better, I read a book, and in the book, the author stated the power of consistency.

As a writer, if you write ten thousand words today and another ten thousand in the next two months, there is a high chance you will still remain mediocre, but if you write five hundred words daily, the odds are that you'll escape mediocrity sooner than you think. Most times, it's not always about intensity but consistency. Small steps often produce big results.

If you wake up every morning and keep doing and believing in your nine-to-five instead of working towards your personal growth and development, then don't expect your financial status to change. Always remember that where you spend your attention is where you spend your life. Making your life better is solely and completely your responsibility, and when you begin to try, help will come. As my mom would always say, when a man begins to make efforts, God starts to help him.

ACTION STEP TO TAKE

1. Find whatever will change your life positively and incorporate it into your daily routine. Do this, and you will be unrecognisable very soon.

RECOGNISE YOUR TALENTS AND GIFTS AND DEVELOP THEM

A seed cannot maximise its potential if it is not buried in the soil. –
Ezedi Souvenir Isaac

Talent is simply any natural ability to do something well; talents are special gifts and abilities that we are born with. Every man has a talent or gift, though some might not have discovered theirs yet.

There's a quote from the Bible that says, a man's gift makes way for him. This statement is very accurate. At some point in life, we find out that we are extremely good at something without having formal education or training in that thing. Many people have become millionaires and maybe billionaires doing what they are naturally good at. Some of these talents could be acting, singing, writing, comedy, drawing, or even sports.

Talents would remain mere talents unless they were developed. There's a saying that constant practice leads to perfection.

Artistic talent is a gift from God, and whoever discovers it in himself has an obligation not to waste it by developing it. You'll be surprised at how successful you'll become just by developing your God-given talents. The likes of Beyoncé have made a fortune doing what they were born to do and are good at.

DISCOVERING YOUR TALENTS

A lot of people face financial troubles because they have not yet discovered their talents. It is easier to become successful with your talents, and here are a few ways to discover them.

1. Ask questions

Ask, and you shall receive. The principle still works. Sometimes, your talents and gifts may be obvious to the people around you but completely obscure to you. So ask people who are close to you what they think your talents are. Write down every response you get, and try to do those things to confirm if you are really good at them.

2. Try to find areas where you excel effortlessly.

In senior secondary school, we were made to choose between the art, science, and commercial departments. A lot of people ignored their passions, strengths, and weaknesses and chose their department because their parents pushed them, their friends were there, or for some other reason. To recognise your talents, you must check and try to determine areas where you excel effortlessly.

3. Meditate

Meditation is an underrated method of achieving whatever you want. This is one of the easiest ways to discover your talents or purpose in life. Sit quietly in a calm room, make sure there is no form of distraction, clear your mind, and ask yourself, what am I really good at, or what was I born to do?"

4. Pray for divine guidance or solicit your creator's help.

If you believe in God or in your creator, this is the best time to seek his help. Sometimes discovering your talents and purpose in life can be difficult, so you need help from a greater and more powerful source. I had a problem choosing a career because I was good at so many things but didn't know what I really wanted to do. I opened up to my mother about this, and the first thing she said to me was, "Pray and ask God. Seek your creator's or God's help and work in line with his wishes, and you'll become an exceptional being.

HOW TO DEVELOP YOUR TALENTS

1. Know your talents.

The first step to developing your talents is knowing them; it is impossible to develop something you don't know. You must recognise your talents before developing them. Many people have not yet discovered theirs, while some people use theirs unknowingly.

One way to discover your talents is to ask yourself or people around you what you are good at. Sometimes, you may not see it yourself; that is why a second or third opinion is needed. The people you should ask are those you spend quality time with, like your friends and family members.

2. Believe in yourself and know that you were never born for mediocrity.

Having the mindset that you were never born for mediocrity pushes you to achieve unimaginable things. You must first believe that you were never born for mediocrity and should work towards developing your talents or gifts, making a name for yourself, and leaving a lasting impact. Soar, because that is what you were born to do.

3. Study successful people who have the same talents as you.

In any field in which you're choosing a career, study the successful people who have thrived in that field. It doesn't matter if they are dead or alive. I'll keep saying and believing that experience is the best teacher because it is, and those who learn from experience are outstanding students. By doing this, you will be learning from other people's experiences, which will place you ahead of your counterparts who have the same talents as you or are in the same field.

4. Study unsuccessful people who have the same talents as you.

I have a very strange habit of studying unsuccessful people. I know everyone tells you to study and learn from the successful ones. We can learn from both successes and failures. I'm always curious to know what made them fail, so I don't end up doing it and getting the same unpleasant and unfavourable result they got. When you study people who failed, you learn what made them fail, what not to do, and what to improve.

5. Practice constantly

I know you've heard the saying that practice makes perfect, and whoever said that wasn't in any way lying at all because it does. It takes ten thousand hours of work, practice, and dedication to master your craft.

The question is, are you willing to commit ten thousand hours of your time to mastering your skill or craft? If the answer is yes and you really desire to develop your talent and become better or even the best at what you do, then you should. It doesn't matter how many minutes you spend in a day; you're moving and will get there. But I'll advise you to put in more time to get there sooner.

6. Seek to improve.

If you have a talent and a very strong and unending desire to improve it, you will definitely become better at what you do. The desire to conquer or evade mediocrity pushes us to great, unimaginable, and seemingly unattainable heights. Develop this hunger to always be better and never relent. There's always a new goal to achieve and a new dream to pursue.

7. Creating value should be your major aim.

Your talents are God's gift to you, and what you do with them is your gift back to God. So it is advised that you use it well. Another thing that pushes you to become the best at what you do is prioritising value creation. When your major aim is to create value and leave a lasting impact, you are constantly motivated to do or get better. I read a post one day that said, "If your business is focused on making only money, then it has failed."

WHY EVERY MAN MUST SEEK TO DISCOVER AND DEVELOP HIS TALENTS

Every man must seek to discover and develop his talents because it is the easiest way to become successful. You can do what you love and are good at and still get paid. It's a win in every area. Rihanna loves singing and has become successful doing that; likewise, John Currin has become a billionaire through painting. It's easier to get rich, famous, and successful using your talents than your skills.

THE MAN WHOSE TALENT MADE WAY FOR

Like I said before, the Bible wasn't lying when it said that a man's gift makes way for him. There was a story of a popular king who was visiting another kingdom. The king of the host kingdom organised performers from every part of his kingdom to welcome his guests. The performers did their best, but none of them seemed to impress the king.

There was a particular man in the crowd who wasn't a performer, yet he had weird abilities. He could twist his nose in a very funny and abnormal way. The king looked through the crowd and saw this young man, and he asked him to come forward and perform on this stage.

In this story, you can see that the man's talent, which some of us might refer to as stupid, weird, or funny, got the king's attention. I've also seen judges on talent shows go wild after encountering talented people.

AFTER TALENT COMES MASTERY

Even if you were born with something and are very good at it, if you don't master it or seek to become better, you'll still end up with mediocrity. For instance, two friends are both good at playing football, but one consistently seeks to improve himself while the other is intoxicated by his so-called amazing skills. It will only take a short time, but the one who develops his skills will surely be better.

My best friend likes football a lot and is a talented football player. He would regularly go for training at a stadium nearby, and the coach at the stadium was very harsh. So one day, I asked him, "Why do you let this coach insult you every time? He replied, "I want to be better at football, and he can help me. It's a small sacrifice for a big goal. I was impressed and learned a very big lesson that day. Sacrifice whatever you can to master your talents.

NO TALENT IS NONSENSICAL OR RIDICULOUS

No idea or talent is nonsense. Believe me, a lot of people have become successful by doing things that look or sound ridiculous. Someone invented a blanket that could be worn, and it raked in over 500 million dollars. The product was known as a snuggie.

A child also makes millions a year from reviewing toys. Your talent can make you successful; it just depends on how well you utilise it, because everything you do in life has the potential to fail or become successful. If you use your talents in a wise or smart manner, success awaits you. Always remember that the person born with the talent they were meant to use will find their greatest happiness.

ACTION STEPS TO TAKE

1. Get a journal or a notebook and write down everything you think you are good at on a piece of paper.

2. Ask people around you what they think you are good at and write it down on a piece of paper.

3. Compare what you wrote down with what your friends say. If there are things on your list that your friends also mentioned, start developing or working to get better at those things. There is a chance that's what you're good at since you mentioned it and the people close to you did too.

CREATE A STANDARD GOAL

Don't force people to know or recognize you, let your success do that for you – Ezedi Souvenir Isaac

Goals are the things you hope to achieve. This chapter speaks not only about creating goals but also about creating standard goals. Without goals and definite plans to reach your goals, you are like a ship sailing without a destination.

The good thing about having goals while striving for success is that even when you are in your weakest moments, trying to give up, or when all hope seems lost, you will have something that keeps you going. You will have this mentality that you cannot stop unless you have achieved what you want. As a child, I set goals for myself that seemed really impossible. I wasn't thinking like the average child, and I wanted things that were beyond my reach. If others could have them, why couldn't I?

Earl Nightingale once said, "People with goals often succeed because they know where they are going. A goal gives you a target and makes you relentless until you reach your goals. It is extremely necessary for every man who intends to be successful to create definite, standard, and smart goals for himself and lay out a blueprint on how to achieve them. There was a time when I was still a broke teenager. I needed a new phone and would do literally anything to get it. Then, I had no money. This led me to embark on a journey and create a very small goal. I wanted to make the most of what I had.

My old phone was in bad condition, but it was still manageable. I wasn't a big fan of menial jobs. At first, I thought this would be a huge constraint on my financial freedom, but it turned out to be my source of motivation and my greatest strength. Being lazy can be an advantage if you're smart. Vusi Thembekwayo once said that if you ask a hardworking person to dig a pit, he immediately starts digging and may not stop till he's done, but when you ask a lazy person to do it, he begins to find something else to do it for him, and from there, innovation is born.

Some of the greatest inventions were made because people found easier ways to do things. I had been hearing a lot about affiliate marketing and had some basic knowledge about it, but I had not taken much interest in it. I didn't have money to afford the expensive courses from the big names in the industry, so I went to YouTube. I watched a few videos, and my knowledge increased, so I decided to practice the things I had learned. I followed top affiliate marketers and documented every single thing I learned.

When I began to practice them, it wasn't an instant success story, and I made a lot of mistakes, but in the end, I achieved my goal. There were times when making sales was difficult, generating leads was difficult, and generating the right leads was difficult, but if you are serious about achieving your goals, only one person can stop you, and that person is you, and you stop by deciding that you don't want to do or achieve whatever you want to do or achieve again.

THE IMPORTANCE OF HAVING GOALS

1. It speeds up your success.

Success is easier when you are specific about the areas where you want to be successful, because when you identify a particular area where you crave success, you work towards becoming better or achieving success in those areas. For example, if you want to become better at running or be a successful athlete, you know that you have to build your speed and stamina. Identifying areas where you want to be successful lets you know where or what to work on. Create a goal, and your success rate will be sped up.

2. It gives you a target.

It's easier to remain persistent or on track when you have a goal. Goals give you something to work for and a solid reason why you should not relent until your ideas and visions have become reality. It helps you determine what you want.

3. Creating goals gives you guidelines to follow in order to achieve them.

The next step after creating a goal is working towards its achievement. Knowing or identifying your goals helps you formulate guidelines to follow in order to achieve them.

4. It improves your discipline and work ethic.

Why do you think some people party and waste their lives while others don't? Those who don't know have something they want and somewhere they want to get to, and it helps them maintain discipline. Discipline is easier to acquire when you know where you are going. Knowing where you're going helps you know what you are doing. To know the route you will follow, you must first know where you are going. So, in order to stay disciplined and develop or maintain a good work ethic, it is necessary to have a goal.

5. Goals increase your focus.

Just like goals help you develop or sustain discipline, they also help increase your focus. When you have a goal, all your money, energy, attention, and time are invested in its achievement.

6. It keeps you motivated.

7. It challenges you to bring out the phenomenal part of you that you probably didn't know existed.

Another important aspect of having a goal is that it challenges you to bring out the phenomenal part of you, you didn't know existed. I never imagined there was a part of me who had the will, courage, and wisdom to earn the large sum of money I did, but like I said, I was literally going to do anything legal to buy myself a new phone at a very young age.

HOW TO ACHIEVE YOUR GOALS FASTER

1. Create a deadline.

One of the ways to achieve your goals faster is to create deadlines. One thing helped me during my career in ghostwriting, and it was deadlines. The first thing I ask a client, even before asking for an upfront payment, is, "When do you need it? It somehow sounds weird that I like shorter deadlines because they push me to do more.

A wise woman once said that goals are dreams with deadlines. Having a deadline makes you persistent and relentless until you achieve your goals. It gives you a sense of competition, not against anyone but against yourself, and generally improves or increases your productivity level.

2. Build discipline.

To achieve your goals faster, you need discipline. Discipline in areas like sex, opposite gender, alcohol and smoking, partying, excess spending, and even around technology Achieving goals is difficult, especially if they are large. This is why you need discipline and endurance to be able to concentrate. Building and maintaining discipline are small sacrifices you need to make for greatness.

3. Start immediately.

A lot of people, especially the old and naive ones, criticise young hustlers and tell them they have absolutely nothing to do with money at their age.

Andrew Tate said that money is more useful when you're young. It is better to have 5 million dollars at age 18 than to have 100 million dollars at age 80. So get up and start working; the clock is ticking, and time waits for no man.

Start early to work towards your goals and create the life you want. The earlier you start a journey; the sooner you will get there. A billionaire once said that one way to predict if a person will become successful or not later in life is the age at which they start. The billionaire is Warren Buffet.

Oprah Winfrey and Walt Disney were two people who dreamed big. Oprah was fired from her job because the producer she worked for felt she was unfit for television, while Disney was fired because he lacked imagination. But these two people had the courage to dream big, create standard goals for themselves, and rise above the limitations that were placed on them.

You should never be afraid to dream big. Those who have gotten to the level you wish to reach are humans just like you, and they have the same organs and the same blood running through their veins. Some might want to say that some of them come from riches, which is not totally true. Bill Gates was the son of a lumberer, and Elon Musk once had a rat-infested office. If they can rise above the barriers placed on them, trust me, you can too.

GOALS AND STANDARD GOALS

There is a big difference between having goals and having standard goals. Goals can be small or big. Moving from 1000 followers to 1020 followers on Instagram is a goal, but a very small one, and becoming a billionaire when you've got no penny to your name is also a goal, but a big one. Create standard goals for yourselves. Standard goals are those that are difficult, look impossible to achieve, or have never been achieved before.

Standard goals normally don't attract support from people. Tell your friends that you are going to be the richest man in the world, and see how they react. I'm certain that 80 to 90 percent of them will laugh at your dreams and mock you. You have to keep going no matter what; every man was created, and a specific duty was assigned to them by their creator. Know that you were never created to be mediocre, and shun mediocrity with every single thing you've got.

Never be afraid to dream big, because you were created to do exploits. It doesn't matter who you are, where you come from, what language you speak, your health status, your age, or your current financial status. Remember, the most beautiful things come from the hardest conditions. See shiny blades and diamonds as examples.

ACTION STEPS TO TAKE

1. Write down a series of standard goals you want to achieve clearly and specifically in your journal or notebook.

2. Write down all the steps you want to take to achieve your goals.

3. Write down all the challenges you're likely to encounter and also write down possible solutions.

4. Write down your expected outcome. For example, "I want to be a super entrepreneur; these are the steps I'll take to achieve my goals. These are the problems I am likely to encounter, and here are possible solutions. In the end, the outcome is that I become a very successful entrepreneur." This will give you a guideline to follow for the achievement of your goals.

CHANGE YOUR LIFESTYLE AND FRIENDS

There are certain kinds of people you will have around you and failure becomes difficult while others make success a tedious task. – Ezedi Souvenir Isaac

Your friends affect seventy percent of the way you think, act, or behave. They can influence your life, either positively or negatively. If you move with people who are more focused than you, there is a chance that your level of focus will increase, and if you move with people who are less focused than you, there's a chance that you might drop to their level.

Having friends is a good thing, but having the wrong kind of friends could be a constraint on your personal growth and progress. It is no new thing that you are the sum total of the people you spend time with. My father once told me the story of a lion who thought he was a sheep. After his birth, his mother died, and he immediately joined a herd of sheep who happened to be passing by at the same time. He lived like them, ate like them, and even behaved like them. One day, the herd of sheep was chased by another hungry lion.

They all ran as fast as they could, including this very lion.

The lion chasing them became very surprised; he had never seen such a thing in his life before. The lion came to hunt again another day, and this same lion tried to run, but he chased him, caught up with him, and dragged him to the nearest river. There he saw himself and what he truly looked like; the lion explained everything to him and told him they were of the same kind. For the first time, he roared, and the mountains shook. This lion thought he was a sheep because he grew up with sheep. This is the same thing that happens to those who move with friends without goals, focus, plans, or even wisdom.

Another example of a lion story with the same lesson is the movie The Lion King. Simba's father told him that the stars were dead kings who were watching over and guiding them, but after he ran away, he retold the stories to his newly found friends, and they laughed and mocked him. This was because they had a lower mindset than him and the people he was around before. If he had told the story to another lion who grew up with lions, maybe he would have understood.

As you move forward in life, you may need to change your friends because everyone around you isn't interested in seeing you improve. The best way to kill a dream or an idea is to tell it to a small-minded or myopic person.

HOW TO CHANGE YOUR LIFESTYLE

There are no steps or guidelines for changing your lifestyle. The only way to change your lifestyle is to study your life and remove anything that is hurting you, preventing you from achieving your goals, or slowing down your goal achievement process. It could be alcohol, friends, women, men, debts, social media, etc.

DIFFERENCE BETWEEN HAVING THE RIGHT FRIENDS AND HAVING LIKE-MINDED FRIENDS

There is a difference between having the right friends and having like-minded friends. The right friends can be like-minded, and like-minded friends may not be the right friends. Assuming you are a thief and you have a group of friends who steal, they are like-minded friends, but they are certainly not the right friends. The right friends are those who help you grow and become better versions of yourself. The right friends support you and criticise you, but they don't just leave it at criticism; they also find ways to make you better. The best categories of friends are like-minded friends, because you will thrive better with them.

ADVANTAGES OF HAVING LIKE-MINDED FRIENDS

1. They will be able to administer help when needed.

One of the benefits of having friends who think at the same level as you is that they'll always be able to offer help, advice, or encouragement when needed. Even if you don't have friends who are as smart or goal-oriented as you, you have friends who support you, and you also have friends who make failure difficult.

Most people may say, "I've been friends with this person for a long time, and I can't let them go now. No one says you have to do it immediately; give them a chance to change their mindset and teach them if they are willing to learn, but cut them off if they aren't. It is necessary for your progress.

2. The level of understanding and tolerance is higher.

Another benefit of having like-minded friends is that their level of understanding and tolerance is higher. I've always wanted to learn chess. At the time, a friend of mine finally volunteered to teach me; another event came up for him. He began to learn cryptocurrency, and whenever I ask him when our next chess lesson is going to be, he is like, "Bro, I'm so sorry I'm busy. I was never offended because I knew he was working towards a better future; this is one of the benefits of having like-minded friends.

A wolf, they say, hunts and thrives in its pack, but it wouldn't thrive so much if some were hunting for prey while others grazed. There is mutual understanding and tolerance when your friends are like-minded.

3. It increases your chances of achieving your goals.

Take your fingers, for example. There is a lower chance for one finger to do what five can do, but when they are all clustered with a common aim, carrying out their task becomes less difficult. Another example is a group of wolves. It is easier for a pack of wolves to hunt and kill prey than for one. This is because of their aligned interests.

Assess your friends and detect those who have no definite plans for their future. Know those who are willing to learn and those who aren't; offer to teach those who are willing to learn and bring them up to speed on where you are currently in life. Also, know those naysayers among them who mock your dreams or ideas whenever you come up with one.

Always remember that one friend can change your whole life. Therefore, find a group of people who challenge and inspire you to do better, spend quality time with them, and it will change your life. A high school boy who was always failing realised it was because all his friends were always failing and decided to do better. His grades changed immediately, and his friends changed.

IF YOU CANNOT CHANGE YOUR FRIENDS, THEN CHANGE YOUR FRIENDS.

The change your friends or change your friends rule translates to replacing your friends with new people who have a better mindset if you have tried changing their characters and behaviours and it didn't work. This is the next course of action you should implement after a failed attempt to change the mindset, habits, or characters of your friends.

Change their lifestyle or replace them. Have friends who discuss goals, ideas, plans, business, health, historical facts, and educational things in general.

ACTION STEPS TO TAKE

1. Assess your friends and try to find out who they really are and what they have done for you. Know those who are supportive of you and those who have a healthy mindset. Also, try to find out about those who are deadweight in your life.

2. Try to change the mindset of those who have a poor mindset and make them better. Give less time and attention to those who refuse to change. It's going to be difficult, but it's necessary.

USE SOCIAL MEDIA TO GROW YOUR INFLUENCE

Instead of pestering people by telling them you built a house, build the house to a high standard and let it speak for itself. High quality products can market themselves. – Ezedi Souvenir Isaac

The world is changing, even though some of us might pretend not to see it. It is also necessary for us to evolve with it and change the way we do things. To me, social media is one of the greatest inventions; it has helped many people grow their influence and even become millionaires. I once read an article that stated that our favourite football star, Cristiano Ronaldo, earns more from Instagram than he is paid by the clubs he plays for. If you are living in Africa or in any other poor country or continent, social media is a powerful and effective tool you can use to combat poverty.

Social media is one of the resources available for you to utilise and transform poverty into financial freedom. The problem with most people is that instead of following the right people or using social media the right way, they prefer to follow celebrities, models, or influencers who do nothing but post photos of themselves in bikinis.

Amy Jo Martin said that social media is the ultimate equalizer. It gives a voice and a platform to anyone willing to engage. This means that social media is accessible to everyone. Another problem with people is that they feel they have to be who they are not before gaining influence on social media, which is not entirely true. There is something unique in all of us that would definitely keep our audience glued to their screens; some of us haven't even discovered it yet, while those who have are ashamed to share it.

WHY SOCIAL MEDIA?

1. It helps you create wealth.

One of the benefits of using social media to create wealth is that it lets you be your own boss and pays you to do what you love. No matter the kind of business you choose to embark on, you need an audience to sell to, and social media gives you that. Our story models are the Kardashian family. It is worthy of note that every member of the family has millions of followers on Instagram, with Kylie Jenner being the most followed. There were unconfirmed reports that Kylie Jenner became the world's youngest self-made billionaire through her cosmetic company. It is also important to note that the majority of her customers come from her social media pages. The same applies to her sisters, who make lots of money advertising for brands on their social media pages. Wealth creation is made easy through social media.

2. It helps you retain and grow your audience.

One of my favourite authors in the psychological thriller genre, Freida McFadden, makes lots of money after the release of her books just by announcing it to her audience. Some even pre-ordered before the original release date. This is because she has been able to hold her audience in one place with the use of social media. If you are an actor, author, or someone in the entertainment industry, utilise social media to retain your audience.

3. You can start, manage, and grow your own business on social media.

Social media has given 2000's entrepreneurs an opportunity that 1900's entrepreneurs didn't have. A lot of businesses now exist only on social media and still make lots of money. It has visibility, lead generation, and marketing tools available for you. The good thing is that they are all in one place and accessible. So if you are an entrepreneur or SME owner, leverage social media.

4. It helps you build connections.

I met some amazing people on social media who helped me grow in several areas of my life. There are certain people you will need to grow with in life, and they might be far away from you or you might not even be able to come close to them in real life, but with social media, it is possible. Your major aim should be to build connections with the right kind of people. Everyone I'm friends with on social media or follow on Twitter is someone I can learn from or someone who can help me grow.

5. It is an easy way to find workers.

Gone are the days when you'll need a plumber, handyman, book editor, or any other form of service, and you'll have to ask someone who knows someone who knows the service provider. Today, all you've got to do is go through social media. I found a large number of the service providers on social media. All I had to do was search for them, check the quality of their past works, and check their authenticity.

Social media can be used in many creative ways. Paul Barren once said, "I use social media as an idea generator, trend mapper, and strategic compass for all of our online business ventures."

An example of a person who has had a lasting influence on social media is Andrew Tate. Though he had been banned on several social media platforms for exhibiting strong masculinity and misogyny, his impact and influence have not declined. There are still thousands of videos about him on Facebook, Instagram, YouTube, and other social media platforms.

You don't need a corporation or a marketing company to brand you now; you can do it yourself. You can establish who you are with a social media following. The key is having a definite niche and great content. Content is fire, and social media is gasoline.

HOW TO GROW ON SOCIAL MEDIA

1. Know the algorithm of the social media platform you choose.

When you are embarking on a journey, read everything you can about your destination. The weather, their laws, political issues, the best hotels, their hospitability and tolerance level, and their food The same rule applies to social media. Every platform has its own algorithm and ways to conquer it. Take time to do research on the algorithm of your chosen social media platform.

2. Do not try to grow on multiple platforms at the same time; focus on one.

Yeah, I know there are temptations. You want to grow on Facebook, Instagram, Twitter, TikTok, and YouTube at the same time. It is good to establish your influence on multiple platforms, but trust me, it isn't easy, and you will get worn out. The best thing to do is focus your time, energy, money, and attention on trying to grow on one or two platforms first, and then you can move on to trying to grow on other platforms. You could even use your audience on one platform to grow the others. This is a premium tip.

3. Do what you are passionate about, love, or have plentiful knowledge of.

So you love tech, but everyone tells you that there is more money in health and fashion influence. Well, if you're going to influence, do something you're passionate about. It will be extremely easy to grow, and if success doesn't come in the early stages, you will be able to endure and remain persistent until it does.

4. Have a definite niche, and do not switch unless you have built a loyal audience.

One thing that can kill or reduce your audience or engagements on social media is audience switching. For example, everyone in your audience followed you because you created crypto-related contents, and all of a sudden you switched to creating contents related to aphrodisiacs. It is great to post memes or jokes sometimes, but please don't overdo it so you don't lose your audience.

5. Study other influencers, including their success stories.

Study influencers or content creators who are doing well; it doesn't really matter what niche they are in. Learn from their experiences, adopt their methods, and try to incorporate them into your social media journey. Also, don't forget to study those who failed and try to discern or understand why they failed.

6. Collaborate with other influencers in the same niche as you.

While collaborating with influencers in different niches might work, it is better to collaborate with influencers in the same niche. It is one of the best and most effective ways to grow your audience. Some influencers experience a situation whereby their post gets to about 1000 people and only 20 people react;

sometimes this is a result of wickedness on the part of the audience, but mostly because of a lack of interest in what the influencer has posted.

It's not about having 10,000 followers; how many people are actually interested in what you're doing? When you collaborate with influencers in other niches, you'll gain an audience, but they might not really be interested in what you are doing.

7. Have good content and be consistent.

There's a popular comedian and content creator in Africa called Sabinus, or Mr. Funny. I went to study his content creation journey, and I realised he conquered with two things: consistency and good content. Consistency will help you become successful, but good content will keep your audience interested and make them return to your page or channel daily. Overall, it has good content. Sometimes, it's not just about doing good, but doing it well.

Here are some of the best social media niches:

1. Health

2. Science/Technology

3. Food

4. Business/making money online

5. Fashion

6. Personal blogs/vlogs

7. Arts

Two sons, upon receiving equal inheritances following their father's passing, took distinctly different paths. One son invested wisely and eventually amassed significant wealth, while the other squandered his inheritance on fleeting pleasures like women and alcohol. Despite receiving the same opportunities at the same time, their choices led them down divergent life paths—one towards financial prosperity and the other towards recklessness.

This story underscores a powerful truth: it's not so much about what we possess but rather how we utilize our resources that truly matters. The same principle can be applied to our use of social media. While everyone engages with social platforms, the way we leverage them can vary significantly. By harnessing social media differently and purposefully, you have the potential to become the person you've always aspired to be. It's not just about having access to these platforms; it's about using them to shape your desired future and create a meaningful impact.

ACTION STEPS TO TAKE

1. If your business exists outside of social media alone, move it to social media. Create a Facebook page, an Instagram business account, or a Twitter account.

2. Challenge yourself to build an audience on any social media platform; it doesn't matter which one.

EXERCISE OR MEDITATE

I earlier mentioned that one of the ways to build confidence is by working out. Well, exercising doesn't just give you confidence; it also improves your mental state, decreases your chances of having bad health, and increases your longevity. It also lets you know that your body is much more capable of doing extraordinary things than you think it is.

Every successful person knows he should exercise regularly to keep a fit body. It is difficult to live up to your potential if your health is failing. Imagine going to close a business deal worth twenty million dollars the same day you have an appointment with a doctor. Exercise eliminates the chances of something like that happening.

Exercise also makes you look better, especially if you're a man. It gives you a better look when you put on clothes. When making business proposals, your appearance matters a lot; it says a lot about you and gives your business partners the mindset that you are not a pauper. Even if you're a woman, it helps you stay in shape. Working out keeps you healthy, and meditation helps you maintain a sane mind. The world we live in is filled with struggles and stress, which is why it is absolutely necessary to maintain your mental state. A few minutes of yoga and exercise won't hurt. The only place where success comes before work is in the dictionary.

Meditation is also important because brilliant things happen in calm minds. If you place a coin inside a bucket filled with water and shake the bucket, you'll notice that it is almost impossible to see the coin, but after the water is settled, you can see the coin. The same thing is applicable to the human mind. Your mind and brain work better when they are relaxed or in a calm state. This is why it is impossible for an enraged or grieving person to make better judgements or decisions.

Learn to work out for at least thirty minutes each day; it must not be complex exercises because you may not be a bodybuilder. It could be early morning jogging or running, running on treadmills, or a few push-ups. I once told a woman she needed to work out, and she said, "I already go through a lot of stress, and that is enough work." This is untrue because stress and exercise are two different things.

Yoga also helps alleviate stress. These are practices you must adopt to become successful. If you interview a hundred wealthy men, you will realise that about 95 of them work out regularly. Another reason why you should work out every morning is because it increases your productivity for the day. Khloe Kardashian said, "I feel so good in the gym that it affects the rest of my day. It's healthy; it's like buying your sanity." Learn to work out regularly; it is a healthy practice.

EXERCISE VS. MEDITATION

The major difference between exercising and meditating is that exercising keeps the body healthy, while meditation keeps the mind healthy and sane.

BENEFITS OF EXERCISE

1. It helps build confidence.

Exercise helps you develop a good body and build confidence. The major cause of insecurity, especially in relationships, is when one partner isn't confident in their body and feels they don't look good. If you want to appear more confident, work out.

2. It improves the tone of your body.

Exercise will give you a good, perfectly toned body. It will help you look good, appear confident and legit before potential investors or business partners, and open more opportunities for you.

3. It keeps you healthy.

This is one of the major benefits of exercising: it reduces your risk of developing a health problem later in life. I admire billionaire Tony Elumelu so much for his ability to keep fit even at an old age.

BENEFITS OF MEDITATING

1. It helps you solve problems, especially the ones that seem difficult.

I can remember when I was younger, whenever I had a problem that looked difficult to solve, my mom would tell me to meditate. The solutions to the biggest problems in life come during times of meditation. Meditation is one way the creator deposits thoughts and ideas into the minds of human beings. If you want to become phenomenal and powerful, learn to meditate.

2. It keeps your mind healthy and sane.

You should resort to meditation if you care about your mental health. Meditation keeps you sane and keeps your mind healthy; this is why yoga is a very good practice for the mind.

BUILD CONNECTIONS

You need people to make money even if you're an armed robber. Honour all men. – Ezedi Souvenir Isaac

Connection means a person or an organisation that you know and that can help or advise you in your social or professional life. I define connections as those people you meet today and build relationships with who have the ability to take you to a higher level tomorrow.

If you want to be successful, build good relationships with lawyers, accountants, business advisors, and bankers. It is very important to have the right kind of connections because you might need them at some point in your business or professional life. There was a time my father had an issue with land he bought, and immediately he called his half-brother, who was a senior lawyer. There is a point in your life when you'll need a particular person to get you out of a particular problem.

IMPORTANCE OF BUILDING CONNECTIONS

One important benefit of building connections with the right people is that it increases your chances of being successful. There was a story of an unemployed young man who got tired of poverty and decided to step up his life. He bought an expensive outfit and a shoe to match with his savings and headed to the most expensive club in his city. He actually did this because he wanted to see how rich people lived.

There he sat down and sipped a bottle of beer that he had bought. After some time, a man who was sitting at the end instructed the waiters to bring him another bottle of beer, which they did. He moved closer to the man and his clique of friends to thank him.

There, he was able to start a conversation with them. He told them of his business idea, and they invited him over the next day. It turned out that they were actually the kind of people he needed to move on to the next phase of his life. This is the power of building connections. Just like Michelle Obama said, choose people who lift you up.

Another important benefit of having or building connections with the right people is that when trouble comes, you'll have the right people who can stand by you. There's little a broken friend can do for you in times of trouble. His financial status makes him invisible to the world and makes people disrespect him. You have to know that the people you know determine how far you go.

Building the right connections is also important because it will decrease your chances of going broke again. If Elon Musk were to go completely broke tomorrow, rising again wouldn't be difficult because he has acquired the skill of making money and, most importantly, he has built the right connections. If you notice, it is very dangerous to have poor friends because instead of raising you up, they pull you down. It may be through their excessive demands or their low mindset.

There are varieties of ways to build important connections, and a few of them include:

1. Attend gatherings or events where rich and powerful people are, and don't go looking like a pauper.

I was watching an interview with Andrew Tate one day. In the interview, he said that one can become rich just by staying around rich people. One of the reasons rich people live in luxurious areas is for privacy, and the other is for connections. I was a member of a club known as the Rotary Club, and they always had events that I attended.

I realised that this particular club was a good way to connect with high-class philanthropic people.

Sometimes, it's never wrong to attend parties hosted by wealthy or influential people because you'll certainly meet people who will help you grow. Networking is a very important part of success because sometimes the people you know determine how far you'll go.

Going to an event hosted by high-class people is one thing, and dressing well for the event is another. I still believe the old saying that one's dressing determines how they will be addressed. Now imagine you're an investor, and a man wearing ripped jeans, earrings, large boots, and oversized shirts walks in with the intention of pitching an idea to you.

Even if his ideas are solid and have the potential to become successful, their dressing has automatically disqualified them because ninety percent of people judge by what they see. Do you know why real estate agents dress classy and look their best? They are trying to give their clients the impression that they are not paupers or scammers and can be trusted. Attend these events and never hesitate to say 'hello' whenever you can.

2. Join golf courses or other sports clubs where wealthy people are, and do not fail to say hello whenever you can.

This is one of the best ways to build connections. Golf courses are always filled with wealthy people. It is often described as a sport for the rich. Join a golf course or any other sport where you are certain you can find connections. You can also become a member of a top gym; a lot of people have admitted to finding wealthy or like-minded people in the gym.

3. Try to build good relationships with your bankers.

Bankers and nurses are mostly rude, especially African bankers, but nevertheless, try to build good relationships with them. Having a banker on your team can open you up to many opportunities and make your growth journey easier. They can be very helpful to you during the times you'll need them if you've established a good relationship with them. You should never underestimate the power of a banker.

4. Find a personal lawyer while working your way to the top.

It is absolutely necessary to find a personal lawyer while trying to build wealth. Most times, it's not just important to have them around to avoid infringement of rights or property or to fight legal battles. They also give legal advice, especially if you're a businessman or a public figure. Go to a lawyer and ask them to become your personal lawyer.

5. Work with or for those who are wealthy.

There's an old African proverb that says, "kings favour those who serve them." The easiest way to become rich is to work for someone who is rich. There was a particular woman who built an empire from the things she carried while serving her boss and his colleagues tea.

Serving rich people helps you establish a certain connection with them, and if you're a faithful and sincere servant, they might reward you. Working with rich people is a great way to build connections because, after you have become financially free, you can proudly say that you know them on a personal level and ask for help whenever you need it.

6. Follow the right kind of people on social media. For example, wealthy businessmen and women, lawyers, and investors.

Some low-profile artists didn't know top artists or have their contact details before they collaborated with them; they simply asked for a collaboration through social media, and when the top musician does research and sees they are legit, a project will certainly be created.

Following wealthy business people, lawyers, investors, etc. and actively engaging in their posts can make them notice you, especially if you are doing something valuable. Social media has made human interaction very easy. I'm an introvert in real life but a very wild person on social media.

Gone are the days where you would need to book an appointment to see a great person; these days you just use social media. Endeavour to follow the right kind of people. My advice is for you to follow mostly those in your niche and related niches. Also, expand your horizons to other niches; one may never know where opportunity will come from.

7. Make friends with those who have the same mindset and strong willpower as you.

Imagine you have three goal-oriented friends who have the same mindset and desire to escape mediocrity as you, and after a while of bustle and hustle, you all become successful in the future. You must have built a very good relationship with them during your years of being friends, and you can confidently call them connections.

I like to build good relationships with ambitious people and offer help to them so that if they eventually become successful, they will be indebted to me, and I can ask for their help whenever I need it. Your friends should have a healthy mindset, a desire to be successful, and strong willpower just like you, so you can all make a phenomenal clique of friends in the near future.

Overall, you have to be honest and present your ideas as soon as you have built a solid relationship. It is not entirely true when people say that rich people only see or notice rich people. They also notice well-dressed, bright-looking, eloquent, and confident people. Sometimes, it is not the amount of money you have that determines how much respect you are accorded but the kind of values you hold. Learn important and well-sought skills and stay valuable. The strength of your network is directly proportional to the strength of your success.

LEARN TO SELL

People only begin to care about the process when they see the results. –
Ezedi Souvenir Isaac

Selling is a very important skill that most people have not mastered, which is why they keep failing in business. Selling means giving something to someone in exchange for money. Selling is one of the most important skills a person can have because it is applicable in every area of life. You can sell ideas, products, services, or even time in exchange for something of equal or higher value.

WHY YOU SHOULD LEARN HOW TO SELL

1. It can be applied in every area of your life.

One important aspect of learning how to sell is that it can be applied in every area of your life and will be beneficial to you no matter what career choice you make. Selling is important in everything we do, and we sell every day. No matter what you choose to do, learn how to sell.

2. It contributes to the growth of your career.

You will do better as a programmer with selling skills than as a programmer alone. Selling will elevate you above your counterparts in the same career and field as you. It is a skill you must develop if you desire more opportunities to be open to you or if you want growth in your chosen career.

3. Selling aids business growth.

With proper selling and marketing skills, there is no doubt that your thousand-dollar business will be raking in millions in a matter of time. I know that entrepreneurs without vision, patience, and persistence fail, but entrepreneurs who are bad at selling or do not have good salesmen on their team fail more.

4. It increases your finances and your chances of becoming successful.

It is almost impossible for a good salesman to go broke because he knows how to make money even from small and worthless commodities. You'll earn for life if you learn how to sell and market. There's a saying that the best salesmen never go hungry or homeless. Selling is a good way to grow your income and finances and achieve success.

5. It is a skill that never becomes outdated.

Centuries ago, becoming a blacksmith was very lucrative, but today blacksmiths are rarely heard of. But since the dawn of time and since the existence of man, we've had merchants and traders. Though the methods of the early men may have been quite different from today's traders, it didn't change the fact that they were salesmen. Selling is one thing that will never become obsolete. We've sold in the past, we sell in the present, and in the future we will sell. This is one awesome reason you should learn sales.

A few tips to sell effectively and make a sustainable income include:

1. Approach customers with the idea of helping them solve a problem or achieve a goal, not of selling a product or service. Every person has something he or she is in need of, and that's where you come in. Offer to help them solve their problems with your products or services, and they will be compelled to buy. This is an effective tip.

2. Know your audience or customer. Imagine approaching a skinny man with fat-reduction products. There is a higher chance that he will not be interested in the product because it is of no use to him. Most salespeople fail because they try to sell to the wrong people.

Also, imagine approaching a man with a pot belly or an overweight woman and marketing the same product to them; there's a higher chance they'll buy it because they need it and not want it. Always ask yourself, who needs my products or services? No matter how effective your products are, they will barely sell if you are trying to sell them to the wrong people. The music is useless if the audience is deaf.

3. Create offers. People tend to like free or cheap things. One strategy for selling is to satisfy them and also make money. Once in a while, create offers, discounts, or bonuses for your customers. Do things like buy one, get one free. Offers help push people into making purchases by convincing them that something is temporarily cheaper.

4. Build relationships. A good salesman must be able to build good relationships with customers. Having a good relationship with your customers increases their trust in you, which converts one-time buyers into

long-term customers. It also enables them to refer you to other people they know who might be in need of your goods or services. Your patrimony level will be higher if you do this.

Let's say you walk up to a random person and try to market your goods to them. They may be uninterested because they do not know you, but if you can build good relationships with people, they'll refer you to other people who need your products or services. Automatically, the trust level will be higher because they have received a testimony or good review about your products from somebody they know. The trick here is that I gain your trust, and you help me gain theirs.

5. Have effective products or render quality services. All these strategies would be a total waste of time if your products or services were poor. Increase the quality of your products or services and watch your business sales skyrocket in no time. If you're a good salesman, you may be able to sell an inferior product to people and make money, but after a while, the bad reviews start coming in, the demand for your products starts reducing, and your business starts failing.

6. Be creative. What differentiates sellers today is their ability to generate fresh ideas. There was a particular bar in the town where I grew up; this bar had customers from different corners of the town, and none else could rival it. Africans, being who they are, assumed they were using voodoo or some other sort of spiritual power.

I decided to observe their customers and their marketing strategies, and I noticed most of their customers were males, and their workers were beautiful and fair young ladies. They also had a sports viewing centre inside the bar. The idea here was to bring men together with what they love most (sports and women) as a marketing strategy and sell to them. Try to be innovative and find new ways to sell, and always try to thrill your customers. Make them happy, and they'll come back again and again until they bring their friends.

7. Be persistent. The fact that you made zero sales yesterday doesn't mean today isn't a good day to try. I learned a valuable lesson from water. Water breaks through the hardest rocks through persistence. It drops and drops on it until it eventually cracks it. The harder you work, the luckier you get. A man once said, "I have never worked a day without selling.

When I believe in an idea, I sell it, and I sell it hard. Always learn to try again and never give up, because the dangerous thing about giving up is that what you want may never happen.

8. Be honest. Nothing kills your business faster than dishonesty. It may work in the early stages, but there's always a repercussion, and it's never a good one. The thing about building a business with lies as its foundation is that even when you come clean, you'll lose the trust of your customers, and they'll hardly give you a second chance.

9. Be brave. Have the courage to walk up to that man and shamelessly promote your product or service. The worst that could happen is that they may yell at you or chase you out, but trust me, there will be a time when they won't be able to chase you out again. Never be ashamed of your hustle because no one will feed you when you're poor. Make your money look dirty and spend it on clean and classy clothes. Life is not about having the right opportunities, but handling the opportunities right. There are so many resources you need to become a good salesman; the problem is that you just don't see them.

It is absolutely necessary for every businessman or woman to learn sales, even if you plan to hire sales representatives, because you'll definitely need the skills one day and it will also contribute to the growth of your business. Always remember that timid salesmen have skinny kids, and the best salesmen are enthusiastic, analytical, delightful, responsive, attentive, and smart.

ACTION STEPS TO TAKE

1. Purchase a course or read books about sales and marketing.

2. For a period of 30 days, study effective selling methods from salesmen and entrepreneurs like Gary Vaynerchuk, Grant Cardone, and Vusi Thembekwayo. You'll need it no matter what career you choose.

PLAN YOUR LIFE AND HAVE A BACKUP PLAN

The best way to make a good decision is to consider the advantages, disadvantages and to see things from different perceptions of life. – Ezedi Souvenir Isaac

There's an old saying that if you fail to plan, then you plan to fail. To me, a plan is a series of steps, especially a written one, that a person has decided to follow in order to get something done properly. The most beautiful and strongest buildings have the best blueprints.

IMPORTANCE OF PROPER PLANNING

One good thing about planning is that it prepares you for the worst. Problems are inevitable in whatever you do. At some point, you'll experience challenges and setbacks. This is why it is extremely important to have a plan, because when these challenges come, you will have foreseen them and prepared for them. One problem Africans have is that they are too religious. Tell an average African that they will experience challenges at some point in their business or professional life, and they'll rebuke them immediately. The bitter truth is that no matter how hard we try to avoid problems; we'll always encounter them. This is why effective planning is important.

Another important aspect of planning is that it makes your quest for success easier. A wise man once said, "Give me six hours to cut wood, and I'll spend the first four sharpening the axe. The task of cutting down the wood would be much easier because of his preparations. This is the beauty of planning.

I have this habit of writing down whatever I intend to accomplish for the day on a piece of paper, and it helps me achieve more. Even before I write a book, I create a very detailed outline of the book, and it makes writing much easier. Praise George said in one of his books that if a person can win on paper, there is a tendency that the person can win in real life.

Planning helps to avoid errors or mistakes. There's always a difference between the execution of an unplanned project and a planned one. During the period of planning, you get to brainstorm useful ideas that would help in the achievement of your goals. Most of the time, a project that was planned is flawless.

There's a saying that if a person doesn't know where they are going, they'll end up somewhere else.

Planning helps us stay on track while achieving our goals. A goal without a plan is just a wish. This is why goals must be followed up with effective planning and definite actions. If your dream is to be a multimillionaire or billionaire, planning will help you stay on track until your dreams are achieved.

Planning decreases the chances of failure and increases the chances of success. I earlier stated that if you can win on paper, then there is a chance that you can win in real life. If you can also win in your imagination, there are also chances you can win in real life. While planning may not totally eliminate the chances of failure because some plans fail, it can increase your chances of success.

There is a story of a young man who went into cryptocurrency because his friend cashed out big on it and bought a car. This young man didn't even understand how cryptocurrency worked and had no plans. To him, it was just buying a coin or token and selling it later when the value increased. Besides ignorance, another problem this man had was pride. He had no prior knowledge of cryptocurrency but didn't want to ask his friend for help. The value of the coin he bought dropped drastically, and he lost his life savings and finally took his own life. It is very necessary to prepare very well for something before we do it. Always look before you leap, so you don't stumble or fall.

It is not enough to have an effective plan. It is also necessary to have a backup plan. Some plans fail, but if you have a backup plan, you can pick up where you left off. The problem with some people is that they trust and believe so much in their plans that instead of believing in your plans, they believe in your goals. Ask yourself, "If my current career fails, what do I do next to become successful?"

While I was in secondary school, we had an exam coming up, and the majority of my classmates were planning to cheat in the exams. While I was studying, they were creating the best strategies for examination malpractice. I didn't want to tell them I wasn't going to cheat in the exams so they wouldn't think I was being overly religious and see me as an enemy, so I kept my thoughts to myself.

The day for the exams came, and things changed. Our exam supervisor got sick, so we had to write our exams in another location (the school hall) under strict supervision from about four teachers. I wrote my exams without much stress while they sat there helpless and disappointed. No one ever expected an asteroid to hit Earth sixty-five million years ago, and no one ever imagined that a pandemic would shake the whole world in 2020. Things can go wrong at any time, and the universe can bail us out. That is why we must be prepared.

A lot of people have solid or standard goals but are terrible at planning. Here are a few ways to plan effectively:

1. Write down your goals or intended projects. You can only know which route to follow when you know where you are going. Big goals require big plans, and small goals require small plans. Write down what you want first, and then try to come up with smart ways to get it. Do this assignment.

Write down the things you want, e.g., the cars you want to drive, the kind of houses you want to live in, the kind of job you want to do, the kind of woman or man you want to marry, the countries you want to visit, the places you want to go on vacations to, the people you'll like to interact with, and the kinds of food you want to eat. Make sure it is detailed information; don't be scared to write down big things.

2. Figure out smart ways to achieve your scribbled-down goals. Look at the things you have written down

and ask yourself, "What must I do to achieve these goals and bring my dreams to reality? Make sure you scribble down every single idea that comes to mind, no matter how stupid or funny it sounds.

3. Analyse the ideas that you've written down. Look at the ideas you've come up with and ask yourself which will be more suitable for the achievement of my goals. It doesn't have to be the most difficult one among them or the easiest one; it also doesn't have to be the smartest or dumbest one, but the most suitable one. After picking the first one, also pick the second and third most suitable ideas and keep them as backup plans. The most suitable idea will be your plan, and the second, third, or even fourth will be your backup plan.

QUALITIES YOU MUST POSSESS FOR EFFECTIVE PLANNING AND ACHIEVEMENT OF YOUR GOALS

1. Courage

To achieve your goals, you must shun fear and be courageous. It takes boldness and courage to do lots of things. To attempt to become successful, you need courage. I earlier mentioned that the most successful people would not have become successful if they didn't have the courage to try.

2.Persistence

Water breaks through rock by constantly dropping on it until it eventually cracks it. This is the power of persistence. Thomas Edison, the inventor of the light bulb, tried and failed many times before he invented the light bulb. Success doesn't always come easy; one may fail multiple times before they achieve their goals. You have absolutely nothing to worry about if you keep trying and become better by learning from your mistakes.

3. Optimism

Something very funny happened while I was sick; my ailment seemed to be getting worse by the day, and everybody was confused. Honestly, I was too, but I decided to remain positive. While everyone lamented and complained about the new symptoms I developed every day, I smiled and said to them, "What if God is actually making my ailment less complex for the doctors to understand by adding new symptoms?

Everyone was confused, and I thought I was just trying to be hopeful. It happened that at that time, the doctors had many assumptions, but my new symptoms helped them become sure. We should learn to be optimistic, but not foolishly optimistic, about every situation. You failed doesn't mean you're a failure. Get up and try again.

4. Self-discipline

A man who has goals stays away from anything that hinders their achievement. These enemies could come in the form of alcohol, women, pornography, or masturbation. The dangerous part about these things I mentioned is that they reduce your mental and physical productivity. Alcohol kills your brain cells, pornography distracts you, masturbation changes your mindset to a lustful one, and the wrong woman destroys you completely. If you're a woman, the wrong man can totally destroy you. This is why you must develop self-discipline and control yourself around these things.

5. Honesty

Dishonesty may bring you favour, but I can assure you that these favours are always temporary and the end result is always fatal. It is absolutely necessary to cultivate the habit of honesty, no matter your profession. Honesty will take you places you can never imagine. I observed that people support and endorse dishonesty, but they also appreciate honesty.

6. Self-confidence

The most attractive quality a person can ever have is self-confidence. It simply means believing in yourself and your own capabilities. Have the mindset that you can do whatever you put your mind to; your mind can do great things, but you limit it. None of us was created to be normal, which is why the creator gave our minds the ability to stretch so we could do extraordinary things.

7. Creativity

That something is being done in a certain way doesn't mean it can't be changed. Find new ways to do things and solve people's problems. Years ago, someone solved the problem of transportation by inventing cars, but a few years later, two people solved the same problem by inventing aeroplanes.

8. Dedication

I read a story about a young man who caught the attention of a beautiful girl in a club. She walked up to him and said, "Hello," but he immediately walked away. If you have goals, you must be dedicated and serious about them. Always give it your best shot.

9. Humility

The reason more people are still poor is because of pride. They try to challenge and criticise those who have made it in life instead of learning from them. One of the ways to become powerful is by serving powerful people, because kings favour those who serve them. Be humble and open your mind to new things.

10. Willingness to learn

Learning never exhausts the mind. In making plans or achieving goals, you must open yourself to new things and have a strong desire for knowledge. Read books, watch the news, buy courses, and be open to mentorship from experienced people.

11. A burning desire to be or do better

Best is the enemy of better. Every day, we should always strive to get better at what we do, even if we are the best in our field. The desire to be or do better unlocks the extra-ordinary part of you, or, as I like to call it, 'the god mode'. I didn't start out as a very good writer; there were so many of my books I deleted after writing because I felt they weren't good enough, but I wanted to be better.

No one starts out perfect; even the great basketball star Michael Jordan missed a lot, but he never stopped and instead sought ways to improve himself. Never compete with anyone; remember, it's you against you. Every day, try to be better than you were the previous day.

DON'T LEAVE PLANS AS PLANS; IMPLEMENT THEM

The thing with a lot of people is that they spend hours planning something they end up not doing. Follow your plans with actions, and success will come to you.

Before you take any action, no matter how small it may seem, learn to make plans. It really helps.

ACTION STEPS TO TAKE

1. Write down everything you want to do—when you want to do it, why you want to do it, and where you want to do it—in a notebook or journal.

2. Write down a series of steps you want to utilize in achieving your goals and the challenges you are likely to encounter.

3. Get to work; you can take the small steps first if it's easier for you that way.

LEARN TO BE PATIENT

The best way to make a good decision is to consider the advantages, disadvantages and to see things from different perceptions of life. – Ezedi Souvenir Isaac

My sister said something to me one day, and it really touched me. She said, "No amount of prayer can make a fruit produce when it's not in season. It is very important to know that great things take time. This is why a ship carrying a lot of goods arrives faster than a speedboat carrying a few people.

Patience is the ability to stay calm and accept a delay or something annoying without complaining. It's not just about waiting; it's about maintaining a healthy mental attitude while waiting. Patience is bitter, but its fruit is sweet.

While I was sick, we tried different options we had to get me back to health, but none seemed to be working. I was confused and frustrated. I was a young boy who had dreams and aspirations, and my ailment was limiting me. Everyone around me advised me to pray and connect with God better. Let's say I did just that, but it was like my creator was silent on me. All I had to hold on to were prophecies from random people on how great I would become; this was a source of hope to me, and I believed joy would come at last. At a time, my family felt I was faking my ailment, but little did we know God was preparing something huge for me.

Many great ideas were born during the time I was sick, and I also learned great lessons that would help me in the latter years of my life during this period. It was during the time of my illness that I discovered who I was. Every pain comes with a lesson, and they do not leave until they have taught these lessons. This is why we must develop patience.

I know of a man who could have become a millionaire crypto trader, but because of impatience and stupidity, he's still an average trader. At the time, this man was being mentored by a cryptocurrency expert. He had a coin that was increasing in value. He went to his mentor and asked if he should sell it. The mentor said no and gave him tangible reasons why he shouldn't. He ignored his mentor's instruction and went ahead to sell his coin to purchase the latest iPhone at that time.

A few months later, everyone under his coach became millionaires except him because of impatience. Note: To lose patience is to lose the battle.

IMPORTANCE OF PATIENCE

1. It improves your mental and physical health.

Some of the health problems we face in life are a result of stress, and impatience breeds stress. They are all connected. You are less likely to experience health problems, especially mental ones, if you can cultivate the habit of patience.

2. It helps you maintain good relationships with people.

Have it in your mind that at some point in your life, you'll meet different kinds of people at different times in your life. This is why it is very important to tolerate people and be patient with them. My elder sister once met a man who hated rinsing his clothes after washing them. This was quite weird to her, but she learned to cope with him. To be successful, you need to build and maintain good relationships with people, and patience helps you achieve that.

3. Patience is necessary for the achievement of your goal.

Every human being needs to understand that something will work, but it may take time. You need to learn the art of patience in order to achieve your goals and maintain your sanity while doing so. Great things take time, which is why a speed boat carrying a few people arrives faster than a ship carrying a large number of people and goods.

4. It helps improve your ability to accept life the way it is.

Not all trees are or will be fruitful. Also, plans will work out, and not all ideas will become successful, but patience allows you to accept life the way it is and keep aiming for the moon. A man who believes in his heart that he will become successful will keep trying no matter how many times he fails or how many years it takes. He knows in his heart that, whether an idea works or not, he'll still make it, so he is patient and lets time do its thing.

5. Patience helps you avoid making quick decisions or choices that may have lasting repercussions.

The cryptocurrency trader in the above story made an irrational decision out of impatience. One thing I have learned in writing is that you shouldn't rush to finish or publish your work. As the day goes by and you go through your manuscript, you realise that you have new things to add and things to correct or remove. The same thing happens with thinking; if you're agitated, you may not think clearly and end up making terrible decisions that may scar you for life. That is why it is very necessary to exercise patience while making decisions or choices.

There was a fictional story about a woman I once wrote. While she was little, a war broke out between her kingdom and a neighbouring kingdom, and this woman was kidnapped and brought to work in the palace of the enemy king. There, she was constantly raped and abused.

One day, a man appeared to her and offered to give her power and dominion over all for fifty years, and in return for the favour, she would sell her soul to him, serve him for eternity, and die miserably. Out of rage, she agreed to his terms. He gave her the power, and she took revenge and killed all those who hurt her, but she gave much more for a little favour. This is an example of the end product of impatience.

6. It improves your thinking capacity.

Our brain works better when our minds are calm; this is why yoga and meditation are endorsed by mental health advocates. Developing patience can help you see things from different perspectives, thereby increasing your thinking and decision-making capabilities.

7. It improves your listening skills.

Patience helps you develop your listening skills. If you are patient with people, you'll listen to whatever they have to say, no matter how senseless or meaningless it may sound. A good listening skill can help you in all areas of your life. So many people fail in life as a result of misinformation, which was forged out of bad listening skills.

8. It increases your persistence level.

If you're patient, you'll keep trying no matter how hard you fail. This is because patience helps you develop the mindset that you will win someday; it could just take time, and all you've got to do is keep trying.

9. It helps in the acquisition of new skills.

I didn't learn forex trading because I didn't have the patience to sit in front of a computer and look at charts all day. Practice makes perfect, but you need patience to practice. If you must learn new skills, you'll need time and patience. It could be being patient while watching long video courses, reading a book, or listening to a boring person speak.

TIPS FOR DEVELOPING PATIENCE

1.Have fun while waiting.

One tip that helps me develop patience is to have fun while waiting. For example, if I'm anticipating something or waiting for someone, I start to play games on my phone or do something I enjoy.

2. Learn to tolerate people.

You can become more patient with people if you learn to tolerate them and their behaviours. I mentioned earlier that you'll go far in life if you learn to tolerate people, because you'll meet different kinds of people at some point in your life. According to William Shakespeare, there are four types of human behaviour: melancholic, choleric, sanguine, and phlegmatic.

3. Practice yoga and meditation.

Life is filled with daily struggles, and adopting a habit such as yoga or meditation can help calm your nerves, increase your thinking capabilities, improve your focus, and, most importantly, help you become more patient. You can even go further by learning a mudra.

4. Learn to control your temper.

The world is filled with annoying people who constantly try to get on your nerves, but you have to remain calm no matter how provoked you are. Learning to control your anger helps you develop patience and stay calm, no matter what phase you're going through in your business or professional life.

5. Be grateful.

Wisdom starts with asking questions and extends to showing gratitude. Learn to be grateful for the things you have and appreciate how far you've come. It gives you a small sense of pride that you can do better and that the best is yet to come, which in turn increases your level of patience.

6. Do things slowly.

You begin to develop impatience when you try to do things as quickly as possible. Some things require more time, effort, and concentration. My father used to say, it is better to do one thing and be good at it than do multiple things and be terrible at all of them.

Learn to do things slowly, if possible, one at a time, and give them your best.

7. In some cases, try to put people's needs ahead of your own.

Selfishness is another major cause of impatience. I was in a bank one day; the bank only had a few seats, and most of the customers stood. The deal was that, immediately after someone got up, the person closer tried to occupy the seat as fast as possible. After a while of standing, I finally sat. I looked beside me, and an old woman was standing. Immediately, I stood up and asked her to sit down. The funny thing was that I was sick during this period.

I'm not saying you should displease yourself to please others, but sometimes try to put others needs before your own. For example, if you're queuing for something, when it gets to your turn, you can ask the person behind you to go first. These little acts develop into habits, and you'll notice that, gradually, you'll become more patient than before.

8. Always try to maintain a calm mind.

I gave an example with a coin and a bucket of water, and I stated how difficult it is to see the coin if you throw it inside the bucket of water and shake it. The human brain functions better when it is calm. Having a calm mind helps you develop patience and cope with whatever comes your way, no matter how tough it is.

9. Find options to help alleviate your stress.

Everyone has things they do whenever they are stressed. Occasionally, I write when I'm angry or sad, watch movies whenever I'm stressed, and pray whenever I'm scared. Find things that calm you down; it could be games, movies, or even interactions with friends. Engage in these activities to relieve stress or anxiety. Remember, only you can perform this task.

10. Play board games like checkers or chess.

I stayed around people who played checkers a lot, and I observed that they were very patient people. Some of them would leave their place of work and play this particular board game until night-time. I found out that scientific research has proven that checkers and chess make you more patient, and chess also makes you smarter.

This fact cannot be doubted because playing checkers made me more patient. I usually take a lot of time to calculate and think of my next move. So, I'll encourage whoever is seeking to be more patient to play checkers or chess. Always remember that the two most powerful warriors in the world are time and patience.

ACTION STEPS TO TAKE

1. Challenge yourself to become more patient and tolerant with people or things.

2. You can start playing games like checkers, chess or any other activity that helps you develop patience.

READ, WATCH OR LISTEN TO THE NEWS AND STAY UPDATED

A woman who reads is dangerous but a man who reads is powerful, he should not be messed with. – Ezedi Souvenir Isaac

There's a study that says watching the news leads to depression. This is not entirely true. The news is divided into different sections, and there are educational and informative contents that you can watch. Knowledge is power, but information is a weapon.

During my final years in high school, I competed in an essay competition I read about on an online news platform. Though I didn't win, I learned a valuable lesson. Listening to or watching the news keeps you informed. There are opportunities that come up every day that you don't know about because you do not watch or listen to the news. There was a study showing that a large number of wealthy men and women used Twitter instead of Facebook and Instagram. This is because Twitter is more of an informative social media platform.

There was a story we read. I read as a child that a poor widow who lived with her children heard on the radio that there was a possibility that the mountain in her village might erupt. Immediately, she rushed to the villagers and told them, but they doubted her, and some even mocked her.

A night before the event, she packed a few of her things and moved to her nephew's house, who lived in another village. As predicted, the mountain erupted the next morning. The village was very small, and everyone in it died. This is the power of being informed.

A similar thing also happened in the days of Noah. God asked him to inform the people he was going to destroy the earth, and when he did, they doubted him. At the end, only he and his family were saved.

IMPORTANCE OF WATCHING OR LISTENING TO NEWS

1. It keeps you informed.

Regularly watching, reading, or listening to the news keeps you informed about the general happenings around you or the events taking place in your professional life. For instance, if you're a cryptocurrency or stock trader, you'll achieve more if you watch the news. It helps you keep tabs on the market in order to know where and where not to invest your money.

2. It helps you retain your value.

I told my mom one day that if she wanted to become rich, she should move with rich people. She replied, "If I go to rich people, they wouldn't even open their gates to me. I laughed and said to her, assuming there is a certain wealthy man whose daughter was kidnapped and you go to him and tell him you have information about his missing daughter, do you think his gatekeepers will open the gate for you or not? I'm very sure they will, and they may even treat you like a king.

Information helps you retain your value, and watching the news keeps you informed. Let's assume you work in an organisation where they have a complicated machine and you're the only one who knows how to operate it. You'll keep getting pampered and respected no matter how many times you misbehave until they find a replacement. They are not respecting you because they want to, but because of the information you have.

3. It broadens your knowledge.

Countless times, I've been told, "You speak like an adult," even when I was a child. I was the only male child in my family and the youngest. My mom had me at an old age. So, I grew up with older people, and I was exposed to a lot of things at a very young age. Two major ones were reading and watching the news. My dad's cousin, who lived with us at that time, was equally old and was a huge fan of newspapers.

I began to borrow them to read, and I became precocious. I also borrowed complex books from my father and sisters. At a very young age, I used words that most adults didn't know the meaning of, and I knew things even my teachers in school didn't know. Watching the news expands your knowledge.

4. It helps you see things from a different perspective.

The best way to make a good decision is to consider the advantages and disadvantages and to see things from different perspectives. The problem with ignorance is that ignorant people only have one point of view, and they defend and endorse their foolish opinions without considering other options. Watching the news helps you see things from other people's perspectives, which in turn helps you make better decisions and judgements.

5. It gives you an image of how other places in the world look; this may help you if you are or are seeking to be an investor.

I've never been to Paris, Dubai, the U.S.A., or Israel, but I already have an image of how these places look. Though some people might argue that they only show you the places they want you to see, a lot of Lebanese people invest in other countries; most of them didn't visit these countries before starting a business there.

Some of them invested in these nations based on what they saw on the news. They might have heard about the nation's good economy, perfect weather, or even good standards of living. Someday, you're going to be big, and you'll invest in nations. Watch, listen, or read the news so you can know the best countries to invest in.

6. It helps you decide what's best for society.

The first step in solving a problem is knowing what the problem is, and if you want to make money, solve people's problems. A lot of products were born just by seeing how people suffered, and a lot of businesses were created to solve people's problems. It is impossible for one person to know the needs of the people, which is why the president has those who represent him at the state and local levels.

Watching the news helps you know where people are hurting, what they need, and where they need it. Let's say you see on the news that a certain community is suffering from drought or water scarcity, and you decide to solve their problem and, in turn, make money by creating boreholes or reservoirs for them. You were able to solve this problem because you first heard about it.

There are various types of news, which include:

1. Business news

This kind of news analyses and interprets the business, economic, and financial activities and changes that take place in society. Basically, it talks about businesses and investments. This is the kind of news I'd advise anyone seeking success to resort to.

2. Political news

This kind of news gives insight into political affairs, but unless you're a politician or have an interest in politics, this isn't really necessary.

3. Cryptocurrency news

This area of news casting gives updates and information about cryptocurrency. Here, you get to learn about coins and tokens increasing or decreasing in value and also keep tabs on the crypto market in general. This is my second favourite.

4. Science or technology

This kind of news brings information about scientific and technical developments or innovations. This part of the news is also very crucial if you wish to stay updated about technological advancements.

5. Sports news

This section of the news speaks about sports like football, hockey, cricket, etc. This is most people's favourite, especially CNN, but it shouldn't be the most prioritised part of the news.

6. Celebrity lifestyle and gossip

Growing up, I spent a lot of time on this part of the news until I realised I was wasting my time. I was busy helping another person stay famous and make lots of money. As a young person looking to become financially stable, flee from this kind of news. Be very selfish with your time; do not spend it on things that will not benefit you. It is only fine to listen to celebrity lifestyle and gossip news if you're a blogger in the same niche.

Here is what I think: it is necessary to read, listen to, or watch the news, but it is absolutely important to filter the content for your own sanity. I would strongly advise you to listen to, watch, or read news related to your chosen career; it is very essential for your growth.

ACTION STEPS TO TAKE

1. Make it your goal to read, listen to, or watch the news every day.

2. Go for contents that are related to business, finance, science, technology, etc.

BECOME A VALUABLE PERSON

Don't crawl if you were born to soar – Ezedi Souvenir Isaac

Value refers to the regard that something is held to deserve; the importance, worth, or usefulness of something. In my opinion, value is that thing a person has that makes him or her sought-after.

Something happened while I was in secondary school: my civic education teacher asked me and my classmates to make a note on a particular topic and gave us a deadline. I was among the few who did theirs, and mine was obviously the best. The day we were to submit it came, and the majority of my classmates didn't do theirs.

They all clustered around me, begging to copy from my note; this was because my civic education teacher was very strict and would not fail to punish them. That day I became a celebrity in class, and even those who didn't like me swallowed their pride because they had no other option. After that day, I returned to being their regular classmate.

The same thing happens in the real world: people with value are sought, respected, and pampered. That is why you must strive to increase and retain your value at all costs. A valuable man rarely speaks of opportunity; it finds him. There was a story of a group of men who journeyed for four days to find one man. This was because their ship was faulty, and only this man could repair a ship as complex as theirs.

THE IMPORTANCE OF BECOMING A VALUABLE PERSON

1. It brings opportunities for you.

A common man dines with lords and kings because he has something to offer them. Becoming a valuable person gives you so many privileges and opportunities that most people don't have or might only dream of. The boat repairer in the story got to travel to another part of the world because of the value he had and what he could offer. If you increase your value, opportunities will chase you.

2. It helps you make more money.

Some time ago, I needed flyers designed for one of my projects. My sister texted a graphic designer, who charged us three thousand naira. I saw some of the guy's designs, and I knew he was very good. I also had another graphic designer who I used regularly, but his price was higher. I went for the guy whose price was higher because I knew his work had no rivalry.

If you're a valuable person, you'll definitely make more money effortlessly. Why do you think public speakers and self-help writers make lots of money? This is simply because they have something valuable to offer.

3. It increases your chances of success.

There is a tendency that a man who has about three different skills will succeed more than a man who has none. If you can strive to be of value, then you're sure of success. Value attracts success.

4. Increasing your value gives you more power and respect.

My brother-in-law said to me one day, "Assuming you live in a town and only you have the phone number of the president of the country and the people know you do, what do you think will happen? The answer is simple: you become a very valuable person in that community. People will respect you and listen to everything you say, and some might even come to you with gifts, pleading with you to speak to the President on their behalf about a challenge they're encountering because you're a bridge between them and a higher authority.

Becoming a valuable person brings you power and respect. Automatically, everyone listens to and respects your opinions, no matter how dumb they might sound.

HOW TO BECOME A VALUABLE PERSON

1. Learn new skills that are in high demand.

Learning valuable and highly in-demand skills like software development, web design, digital marketing, copywriting, programming, search engine optimisation (SEO), social media management, sales, and marketing can increase your value and place you in the top spot. Whatever job you take, make yourself valuable, then indispensable.

2. Read books

When we read, we unlock concealed or unknown information. I never had a degree in business, and I don't plan on getting one. I started my entrepreneurial journey as a child and improved myself with books. I read books like Think and Grow Rich, Start from Where You Are, Maximising Your Potential, Rich Dad, Poor Dad, Knockout

Entrepreneur," etc. I made efforts to implement the things I read in these books. At some point, I began to speak and act like an adult, even as a child.

A man who has valuable information is a valuable man. I gave an illustration when I talked about going to a rich man with information about his kidnapped child. Imagine you found gold, and everyone knows you found gold but does not know the location of the gold. Trust me, you'll get the best treatment from even the most hostile people until you divulge the location. Valuable information makes you valuable, and books give you valuable information; that's how it works.

3. Regularly work to improve yourself.

The enemy of better is best. Best doesn't mean there isn't room for better. My father was a sesquipedalian; he would regularly read and learn new words, even at an old age. To me, retirement was a time for one to rest before transiting to the world beyond. I realised that my father was trying to improve his vocabulary, and he was getting better by the day.

Most people think they shouldn't strive to be better because they are the best, but it is very important to know that you can never be the best at something.

Either someone better has not been born or discovered. So, if you think you're the best, endeavour to be better, and if you think you're the worst, endeavour to be better.

4. Solve people's problems.

If you've seen this movie, Bahubali, you'll notice that the people praised him after he carried a shivling on his shoulder. For that moment, he was their God because he had solved a problem for them. If you want people to value you, find an issue plaguing them and provide a solution for it. Even if you can't attempt it, it gives them the mindset that you have them at heart, and in return, they begin to value you.

5. Grow your network.

The more notable or important people you know, the more valuable you become. One of the benefits of this is that you can make it big just by connecting people. Make friends with lawyers, bankers, businessmen, doctors, and even influencers. Always seek to grow your connection and watch your value increase.

While two friends were in university, one was learning new skills alongside the formal education he got, making himself valuable, while the other was invested in getting a good GPA. One graduated and became a multimillionaire. I think you know which one.

ACTION STEPS TO TAKE

1. Challenge yourself to learn a new skill. Spend at least one hour every day trying to learn and master that skill.

2. Seek to build a network of friends in relevant fields. You can utilize social media for this. Establish a strong relationship with them.

BE WILLING TO LEARN FROM YOUR MISTAKES

Since mistakes are inevitable, why not learn from them? – Ezedi Souvenir Isaac

Mistakes are inevitable in life, but what actually counts is what we make out of these mistakes. No matter how hard we try, we can never change the past, but we can hold on to lessons from it. At the time I was sick, my mom took me to a spiritualist out of pressure. We were told that whatever I was suffering from had ties to the spiritual world, and because our minds were disturbed, we believed. We were core Christians in my family and had never practiced any other religion before.

We got to the spiritualist's house, and after some divination, we were told I was under attack from a witchcraft coven. We got some materials as instructed by the spiritualist, and a ritual was carried out to free me from the acclaimed torments of the witches. During the ritual, I was asked to step on an exploding substance, and it scarred me for life. Some parts of the soles of my feet were burned.

I could not go back in time and change the past or magically make the scars go away, but I learned a valuable lesson. Never seek solutions in places where you won't find them. No one is born perfect, and no one who is good at whatever they do was born that way; they all learned, made mistakes, and grew. One thing you should always have at the back of your mind is that growth is a process, not an event.

Sophia Loren once said that mistakes are part of the price one pays for a full life, and I believed her. If Mark Zuckerberg had waited to learn about social connections before he created Facebook, it would have remained a dream. I'm happy whenever I make mistakes because I know that will be the last time I make them. A person who doesn't make mistakes doesn't try new things.

THE BENEFITS OF MAKING MISTAKES

1. It helps you learn.

I love to try novel things; sometimes I fail, but I learn new things and new ways things should be done. As a child, I was very handy with tools and could fix electronic gadgets without any formal knowledge. It would interest you to know that I learned by trial and error."

Trial and error means testing out numerous options when trying to solve a problem. Trial and error is very risky because whoever is implementing this strategy knows that there is a probability that whatever they're doing might not work, yet they move on to do it. The trick here is that whenever I try to repair these things, I make mistakes, and automatically, it registers in my head that I shouldn't try that method any longer. Mistakes are very good teachers, but you must be willing to learn.

2. It helps you grow.

Mistakes help you grow and become better. If you're scared of making mistakes, then there's absolutely no way you can grow and become better. I told you earlier that growth is a process, not an event. You don't become better overnight, but with constant trials, mistakes, and failures.

3. Some amazing and innovative things were the product of mistakes.

I bet you didn't know the pencil eraser was invented by mistake. A man called Edward Nairne picked up a piece of rubber instead of bread crumbs and discovered that rubber had erasing properties—a genius invention borne out of a mistake.

A lot of other products, like penicilin, potato chips, cornflakes, fireworks, and even microwaves, were reportedly created by mistake. Making mistakes helps you try out new things, and in the process of trying out new things, something extraordinary could be created.

4. It increases your experience in your chosen field.

Experience is the best teacher, and those who learn from experience are outstanding teachers. If two businessmen were standing before me, one a fresh graduate with a degree in business and the other with ten years of experience in business, if I were seeking mentorship, I'd go to the one with ten years of experience. Because, over the years, the second man has grown by learning and making unforgettable mistakes, if I were to learn from him, I wouldn't make the same mistakes he made and may only move on to make new mistakes.

5. Mistakes put you ahead of others.

I chose the second man in the example I gave above because he has made mistakes and gained experience. Mistakes increase your experience and put you ahead of others. The best programmers and software developers learned and became better—maybe the best—by making mistakes.

6. Mistakes make your success sweeter.

There's a feeling you get when you finally do something right after multiple failures. Imagine how Thomas Edison would have felt when he successfully invented the lightbulb after many failed attempts. Knowing you were able to make mistakes, fail, try again, and eventually win is amazing, and it encourages you to try out bigger and better things.

7. It makes you stronger.

Some criminals become more hardened after returning from prison; this is because they've gone through many hard conditions, and as a result, they've become tougher. I once invested in a Ponzi scheme called 86FB. My sister introduced me to this platform, and without much questioning or research, I put my money into it.

Eventually, it crashed, and I lost my money. It was disheartening at first, but I learned a lesson: never invest in such things again. This was not the only benefit of this terrible mistake, because I learned how to deal with business losses without losing my sanity.

I've invested in many things that didn't work out, but I don't sit in one place dwelling on the past; I move on to the next and try to do better. The more mistakes you make, the stronger you become. The toughest people you see come from the harshest conditions.

8. Mistakes make you wiser.

One amazing quality about me is that I never make the same mistake twice. I asked myself one day, "Why do people go to old people for advice when there are many who are younger and probably wiser? One of the reasons I asked this question was because I felt foolish people could also grow old. I got the answer after a while of pondering.

People are automatically wiser in old age because they've seen many things, tried many things, made mistakes, and even failed. Mistakes make you wiser because you learn not to repeat the same old things that didn't work or change certain things so the same old things can work. Take chances and make mistakes. That's how you learn. Remember, mistakes grow your brain and are part of the price one pays for a full life.

ACTION STEPS TO TAKE

1. Write down every costly mistake you've made in life on a piece of paper.

2. Write down the lessons you learned from these mistakes and put them beside your bed. Find a quiet place and read it out loud in such a way that it sinks into your head. You'll never make that same mistake again if you do this.

BE PERSISTENT

Persistence is a very powerful tool because the more you try to do something, the more you figure out how to do it properly. – Ezedi Souvenir Isaac

There is no magic to achievement; it's really about hard work, choices, and persistence. Calvin Coolidge said, "Persistence and determination alone are omnipotent."

The first definition of persistence that popped up on my phone's dictionary when I searched it was 'obstinately refusing to give up or let go.' In simple terms, obstinate means stubborn. If you must be successful, you must learn how to be persistent. Steve Harvey once said that "If you give up, there is a probability that what you want might not happen. This is because persistence guarantees that results are inevitable.

Now imagine that Thomas Edison had stopped on his 98th trial while attempting to invent the light bulb or that J.K. Rowling had given up after having her books rejected. I had the inspiration to write down a particular quote that came to me one morning. I wrote, "When you are persistent enough, stubborn and resistant things lose their ability to remain stubborn and eventually succumb to your will."

Water cuts through rock not because of its power but because of its persistence. There was this parable about a persistent widow in the Bible. There was a judge in a kingdom that feared neither God nor man, and there was a woman who came to seek justice from the judge. The woman troubled the judge until he was forced to give her justice (Luke 18:1–8).

BENEFITS OF PERSISTENCE

1. It increases your chances of success.

Let's assume two women go to the gym, both with the intention of gaining better shape. Along the way, one stops because she feels it's difficult, while the other continues, spending at least five times a week in the gym. Who has a better chance of attaining the body they both seek? My bet is on the woman who is persistent no matter what.

During my writing journey, a man told me that if I must become successful, I should embrace consistency and persistence no matter what. Steve Harvey once said, "If you give up, the guarantee is that what you want might never happen." The more you try, the better your chances of becoming successful. I told you before that I don't think we would have light if Thomas Edison had given up on his 98th or 980th attempt. When asked how he felt about his failure, he replied, "I have not failed 1000 times. The light bulb was invented in 1,000 steps. Keep going no matter what; trust me, you're learning and growing.

2. It can increase your expertise.

The great NBA player, Michael Jordan, missed more than 9,000 shots in his career, yet he is one of the greatest basketball players of all time. Mistakes and persistence are two things that can greatly increase your knowledge in a particular field. Mistakes can help you get better, and persistence can help you become successful.

3. It helps you learn about your shortcomings and fix them.

When you're persistent at whatever you do, you'll have enough time and opportunities to learn your weak points. When I started writing as a child, my spelling and sentence construction abilities were very good, and I was very creative, but I had only one problem. My punctuation was terrible. I didn't take any English courses on how to punctuate properly, but I figured things out myself and got better. The thing here is that I learned that my punctuation was poor through persistence and fixed it through persistence. Persistence is a very powerful tool because the more you try to do something, the more you figure out how to do it properly.

4. Persistence will place you above your rivals.

In my illustration above, the two women began to work out at the same time, but one has a higher chance of attaining the figure she wants because of her persistence. Persistence helps you become more skilled and experienced, which will put you ahead of your equals and superiors.

5. It shows how ambitious a person is.

One way to get favour and support from wealthy people is to be serious about what you do. Many people will not help with your business start-up but will immediately start supporting you when they see how serious you are by being persistent. This is why most businesses do not attract investors in their early stages; the investors want to know if the business has come to stay and if it has the potential to grow. The stronger your never-giving-up attitude is, the more ambitious you are, and the more ambitious you are, the more support you get.

HOW TO BECOME PERSISTENT

1. Never accept NO for an answer.

If J.K. Rowling had listened to "no" from the publishers she sent her manuscript to, then maybe the Harry Potter series wouldn't have existed. The word "no" has thrown so many people into depression, anxiety, and sadness because they never learned to take it.

The fact that you were rejected simply means that you were built for better. I've seen a lot of entrepreneurs get rejected on Shark Tank and move on to grow their businesses. One simple way to take the word "no" is to keep going no matter how many times you get rejected, as long as you believe in your dreams or ideas.

2. 'Impossible' should be a non-existent word in your vocabulary.

A woman once said that there is nothing like the impossible, and even the word itself says, "I'm possible." If you must become successful, you must get rid of the word impossible. Nothing is impossible.

If you had told the people of the fifteenth century that in the future we would have objects that could move people and goods just by running on liquid, I'm sure they would have doubted it. As the day goes by, you realise that those things that seem impossible are actually possible.

3. Always believe you were born to be an eagle, not a parrot.

Why should you be a pigeon or a parrot if you were born to be an eagle? Every human being is capable of doing great things, but somehow we choose mediocrity and commonality because it's easier. There are numerous stories of people who have done amazing things in the face of danger. They blame it on the adrenaline rush, but in reality, their bodies have always been capable of such great things; they just needed a trigger.

Always endeavour to be the best version of yourself. The human mind is powerful and unpredictable at times. In whatever you do, keep in mind that you were born to create history and not just be part of it. Until you learn you were created to do and achieve more, you'll never access the extraordinary part of yourself.

4. Know that your mind is capable of doing great things.

Napoleon Hill said in Think and Grow Rich, "How powerful is the human mind? It builds or it destroys." I believe my creator built me to be phenomenal, not mediocre; that is why he gave my mind the ability to stretch limitlessly. Always remember that you can do anything; you just have to put your mind to it.

Believe in the exceptional power of your mind. Your mind controls your body; if you make your mind understand that you were created for greatness, it will pass the same information to your body, and you'll be surprised at how much you will be able to achieve relentlessly. This is one trick to becoming persistent.

5. Find a source of motivation.

My biggest source of motivation was my mother, but I also had other sources. One day, I went on the social media application called Pinterest and downloaded two pictures, one of a lion and the other of a Rolls Royce. I used the photo of the lion as my home screen wallpaper.

The purpose of the lion was to remind me that I was an extraordinary person and I could do anything I put my mind to, and the purpose of the Rolls Royce was to make me conscious of the fact that I hadn't driven in a Rolls Royce yet and must keep hustling. These were my sources of motivation. The major importance of having a source of motivation is that you have something that keeps you going when things get tough or when you feel hopeless. Find a source of motivation; it could be a person or even an object.

6. Be confident in your abilities.

The first step in achieving anything is believing you can get it done. Self-confidence is one of the most amazing qualities a person can have. A mechanic starts repairing a car because he believes he can, and no matter how many times he fails to discover the fault, he keeps trying because he believes he can fix the vehicle. If you have faith in your abilities and believe you can get things done, you'll keep trying no matter how difficult it gets or how many times you fail. From there, persistence is born.

7. Read stories or watch documentaries about successful people.

One good way to stay motivated and persistent is to read stories and documentaries about successful people, especially those who built their empires from scratch. Besides self-help, two other types of non-fiction books I love are memoirs and autobiographies. When I read these books, I get to learn from the author's life experiences.

Growing up, I also watched documentaries about wealthy people and shows centred on rich people. Besides action movies, I also watched films like Undercover Billionaire, Wolf of Wall Street, Rich Brother, Poor Brother, etc., and some reality shows like Million Dollar Listing. These things helped develop my mind. I felt that if these people could rise above the odds placed on them, I could too. I just have to keep trying, no matter what.

One beautiful thing about persistence is that even if you don't emerge as the best at whatever you do or don't achieve what you want, the fact that you didn't give up is delightful, and it encourages you to keep trying other available opportunities. Challenge yourself to keep going no matter how tough your journey becomes, and you will be gleeful with the end product.

ACTION STEP TO TAKE

1. Every single day, tell yourself that you will never give up until your goals and dreams lose the ability to remain stubborn and resistant and succumb to you.

BE PRAYERFUL OR HAVE A SPIRITUAL BACKUP

The easiest way to be happy is to accept everything you have in good faith but the most difficult way is to know you're built for more and work towards achieving more. – Ezedi Souvenir Isaac

Having a spiritual backup eliminates the chances of your problem being spiritual. The physical cannot combat the spiritual; only the spiritual can combat and control the spiritual. A spiritual backup is supernatural, extramundane, or divine guidance and protection that a person has.

A man's business began to fail; his marriage was on the verge of breaking up; and his whole world was crumbling. People around him began to fill his head with ideas that his problems were from a spiritual source, and some even offered to refer him to strong spiritualists, but this man refused; he was firm on his decision and kept saying one thing: "I know the God I serve; he never fails. The people around him thought he was being stupid, while others felt he was only being stubborn.

After a while, his life began to get back into shape, and everything that was broken became fixed. This man knew his problems were not spiritual because he believed in the God he served.

At some point in our lives, we will experience something that looks paranormal, if we haven't already. I'm a core believer in spirituality, and I also believe in God. I know that great evil exists in the world, even though we try to cover it up so we don't sound 'fetishistic'. When you wake up every morning, dedicate yourself to the being you serve and ask for divine guidance and protection. This is one way to make your day successful. Always know in your heart that there are some things you cannot control, no matter how hard you try.

As Christians, we believe in God and the power of prayer. Prayer is simply a mode of communication between God and man or between the creator and his creations. Muslims also believe in the power of prayer, as do many religions across the globe. When we pray, we are simply dropping our egos and accepting the fact that we need help dealing with certain challenges.

The power of prayer should not be underestimated. When we pray, we solicit and get help from a divine source. If you are a Christian, Muslim, or from any other religion that believes in the powers of prayer, never underestimate the power of prayer.

WHY WE NEED SPIRITUAL BACKUP

There is a certain ornament I used to like. It is widely known as the evil eye bead or Nazaar amulet. I was very curious about this particular piece of jewellery and decided to look up its meaning and origin. It turned out that its major use was to repel negative energy from envious or dangerous people and beings. This particular ornament has been around for thousands of years, meaning evil has always existed. We need spiritual backup because:

1.There is so much evil in the world.

No matter how hard you try to please everybody, there are still people who will not like you or appreciate what you do. It could be a result of envy or hatred. Having a spiritual backup prevents this evil from reaching or harming you.

2. It eliminates the chances of your problem being spiritual.

The first step to solving a problem is knowing the problem and its cause. If one does not know his problems or their roots, odds are they will not be able to find a solution. This is why doctors ask for a detailed explanation of your symptoms.

3. Sometimes, you will need help from a supernatural source in order to succeed.

Sometimes, you will need help from a spiritual source if you want to succeed in life, especially if you're starting from scratch. Prayer was my own way of soliciting help from God, even though I wasn't praying regularly. There are some things you cannot do or achieve unless you have supernatural help.

4. You become divinely protected.

If you have a spiritual backup, you are shielded against certain attacks. Some people walk and act with so much confidence and bravery because they know and believe that there is not one thing anyone can do to harm them. Spiritual backing prevents fear, helps you maximise your potential, and helps you be or do the best you can.

WHY WE MUST PRAY

Praying is a way of requesting spiritual backup. The same reasons we must have a spiritual backup are the same reasons we must pray. The main reason you should pray is because prayer is the only method of communication between man and his creator.

HOW TO PRAY

Here is one tip to get your prayers answered, especially if you are a Christian: put other people's needs before your own. God likes compassionate people. Your first five prayer points should be centred on other people; they must not also be family members. Pray for other people.

There are many things you cannot achieve without a spiritual backup. Here is my advice: no matter what religion you practice, honour the God you believe in and watch things fall into place for you.

ACTION STEP TO TAKE

1. No matter your religion, make it a habit to pray every day and honour your creator in order to tap help from an extra-mundane source.

LEARN TO JOURNAL AND DOCUMENT YOUR EXPERIENCES

A man cannot achieve anything if he doesn't have something pushing him to. – Ezedi Souvenir Isaac

Learn to journal and document your experiences. I love to express myself on paper because it won't mock, laugh, or even pity me. It just alleviates my pain. Journaling is one great thing that is often underestimated.

Most people do not understand its power. I told you in the beginning of this book that a journal is like a garbage can where you can empty the trash in your mind, like negativity, thereby enabling you to achieve a better mindset. I also told you that I sleep with four notebooks on the same bed: one for my feelings, one for my quotes, one for my ideas, and one for outlining books I'm writing or intend to write.

Through journaling, I evacuate negativity and bad energy from my mind and scribble down ways I can improve my life. There are varieties of things that could be journaled about; they include ideas, feelings, plans, opinions, life lessons, your daily experiences, and your goals.

HOW TO JOURNAL

1.Get a journal and a pen.

The first step to journaling is to get a journal or notebook and a pen. If you are comfortable with digital methods, find software that helps you journal. I believe in and prefer the traditional method of using pen and paper. Find whatever works for you.

2. Document your experiences.

I like to document every one of my experiences so I can tell the stories later and they can serve as an inspiration to others. Documenting your experience helps you know how far you have come and where to improve. Improvement requires you to keep track of your progress and know where you are experiencing difficulties.

3. Write down how you feel at all times.

Another way to journal is to write down how you feel at all times. There's a kind of heavy weight that is lifted when you share your problems. Journaling gives you an avenue to pour out your feelings and express yourself.

4. Scribble down the things you intend to achieve for the day.

The best way to get things done is through proper planning. If you want to achieve more, create a timetable and write down the things you want to achieve for the day and the time you want to do so. It helps you get a lot done in a short time. At the end of the day, review it and see how much you have achieved for the day. It also helps you know whether you are making progress or not.

5. Write down every idea that comes to mind.

I can remember people and events, but I have a problem remembering ideas. This is why I always have a small journal, a pen, or my phone with me. Ideas are very slippery, and that great idea could leave your mind in a twinkle of an eye. While others may return when something triggers your mind, some remain lost forever. Always write down every idea that comes to you.

IMPORTANCE OF JOURNALING

1. It helps you find clarity.

Journaling is a great way to preserve your mental health and find emotional peace. A burden is always lifted when we journal, and it helps us find peace and mental clarity.

2. It relieves stress and anxiety.

Journaling is a great way to alleviate stress. At the end of every day, pick up your pen and your notebook and write down every single thing you experienced that day; it doesn't matter if it was good or bad.

3. It helps you know the areas where you need to improve.

You cannot find a solution if you don't know the problem. Journaling will help you discover the problem and know where to improve. It's easier to find your faults when you document everything you do. Once in a while, go through your journal and try to figure out where you've made mistakes.

4. Journaling reminds you that you haven't achieved your goals yet.

One way I achieve a lot and make my day useful is to write down things I want to do, open the page where I wrote them down, and keep them beside my bed. The reason is because I'm an introvert and I rarely leave my room.

So whenever I start becoming distracted, I look at the open book on my bed, and I'm reminded I've got things to do. The same thing can be applied to your life. Journaling will make you goal-oriented, and there's an incomplete feeling you'll get when you see that the things you penned down haven't been achieved yet. It moves you to do or achieve more.

5. It gives a series of steps you can take to achieve your goals.

The best way to plan your life is to lay it out on paper. When making plans on paper, don't just write what you intend to achieve. Write down how you intend to achieve it, why you want to achieve it, and the problems you might encounter on your journey. Try to solve the problem on paper as you would in real life.

6. A journal is like a companion; it's always there for you when things get tough.

A journal is a great friend, especially for those who have trouble expressing themselves. Why I like journaling is that I tell it everything and it remains a secret. Sometimes, when life gets tough, take a moment to read your journal, and you will see how far you have come and have a reason to be grateful.

7. Your journal today could be another person's guide to success tomorrow.

After my father's death, I was going through his documents one day. I discovered a notebook where my dad wrote some of his life's experiences, and I learned some important lessons there. The journal you write today could be someone's source of hope tomorrow, and your story could become one that inspires people and places them on the path to success.

ACTION STEPS TO TAKE

1. Get a journal or notebook and a pen.

2. Write down about twenty or more.

3. Write down your sources of motivation. Motivation is quite different from inspiration.

4. Write down people that inspire you (successful people).

5. Write what you want to achieve in life:

    i.   Where you want to be
    ii.   Things you want to own, e.g., cars, houses, landed properties, gadgets, etc.
    iii.   Class of people you want to mingle with.
    iv.   Type of places you want to visit (for business, vacations, shopping, or other purposes)
    v.   Kind of spouse you want to have.
    vi.   Type of charity you want to do.
    vii.   Kind of life you want to give the people around you.
    viii.   Kind of wealth you want to leave behind for your coming generation.
    ix.   Type of power and influence you want to have in society.
    x.   Kind of legacy you want to leave behind after transiting.

6. Write down how you intend to achieve them.

7. Write down how you plan on making your dreams a success.

8. Write down the things that limit you.

9. Write down how you plan on breaking these barriers and tackling these limitations.

10. Every single day, tell yourself that you will never give up until your goals and dreams lose their ability to remain stubborn and resistant and succumb to you.

11. No matter your religion, make it a habit to pray every day and honour your creator in order to tap help from an extra-mundane source.

12. Finally, write, "I (your name) was created to be exceptional; I was born to soar and not crawl, and I can achieve anything I put my mind to.

By doing this, you'll be able to live your dream life first on paper, which will help you live it in real life. The reason is that if you succeed on paper, there's a tendency that you will succeed in real life. Therefore, achieving whatever you want will be less difficult because it's going to feel and look like you have actually done it before.

SEEK TO REGULARLY IMPROVE YOURSELF

What you do every day either brings you closer to achieving your goals or pushes you away from your goals. – Ezedi Souvenir Isaac

I'm not the best person, but as the day goes by, I search for ways to improve myself, thereby improving my life. I constantly take courses, read books, and even ask questions. I told you before that best is the enemy of better. No one is born perfect, but the good thing is that we were built with the ability to improve.

I had a classmate in secondary school; I was a faster runner than he was and always beat him in every race. Then one day, we began to argue, and I told him I was a faster runner than him. He was like, "That was before and not now. In fact, I challenge you to a race. I stood up with so much pride and confidence that we headed to my school's field. The race started, and to my greatest surprise, I couldn't catch up with him. This boy was desperate to be better at running and trained so hard. On Saturdays, he would go for a race, train in a local stadium that was in my town, and practice tirelessly. He sought ways to improve himself while I sat there, deceived by my little wins.

I have no problem with formal education; in fact, I'm a big fan, but my only problem is that schools don't improve. The same curriculum that was used ten years ago is still being used today. I believe that subjects like financial management, investing, cryptocurrency, coding, and other digital skills should be added to our secondary curriculum. By so doing, we will not only be raising literate men and women who can speak for themselves and make sound decisions, but we will also be raising financially free individuals.

WHY YOU SHOULD IMPROVE YOURSELF

There's only one reason I think everyone should strive to improve themselves. I know and believe the creator built us for exceptionality, not mediocrity, but to access this great version of ourselves, we must seek to improve ourselves and our lives regularly. A seed cannot maximise its potential if it is not buried in the soil. You cannot also become the extraordinary being you were created to be if you do not work towards it.

HOW TO IMPROVE YOURSELF

1. Read books.

I explained the benefits of reading with what I called the stiff neck theory. A woman who reads is dangerous, but a man who reads is more than dangerous; he should not be messed with. This is because you don't know what kind of knowledge he has tapped or from what source he tapped it. The best, greatest, and fastest way to improve your life is by reading. Ninety-eight percent of successful people are avid readers. Read books that are in the self-help genre if you intend to get your life in shape.

2. Watch knowledge-instilling shows and documentaries.

A lot of successful people will tell you that watching television will not help you grow. Well, that's a very big lie; the real thing is that watching the wrong content will not help you grow. Everything around us has the capability to make or break us. It solely depends on how well we utilise them. A lot of people have become millionaires through their smartphones, and a lot of people have died because of their smartphones. You just have to do things a little bit differently to attain success. I recommend shows like Undercover Billionaire and Wolf of Wall Street for anyone who desires success.

3. Learn the act of gratitude.

I told you before that you'll start receiving new and better things when you begin to appreciate what you have. Gratitude is very important in whatever you do; never hesitate to say, "Thank you, I'm grateful, or I sincerely appreciate," whenever you can. Sometimes, we don't appreciate what people do for us because we feel it is small.

One thing you should understand is that when people give you a gift or do you a favour, they have either given you a portion of their twenty-four hours or their money. For me, the best gift I can give to people is my time, because I value my time more than anything else.

Another reason we don't practice gratitude is because we feel there's nothing to be grateful for. I began to appreciate good health, strength, a good appetite, and the ability to walk and see clearly during the period I was ill. Be grateful, no matter how small the favour might seem. Be grateful for being able to wake up every morning, being able to think, talk, and plan, and being grateful for your loved ones.

4. Ask questions

Wisdom starts with asking questions and extends to showing gratitude. If I don't understand something, then nothing can stop me from asking questions. We were not created to know everything, but we were built with the ability to learn and grow. As a child, I asked lots of questions, and I became wiser.

There are so many things you will never know until you cross over to the world beyond, unless you ask questions. Knowledge and wealth are two things that are always available to us; all we have to do is desire them, and if our desire is strong enough, we will definitely get them. Your life will start to take a positive turn, and you will understand so many things if you learn how to ask the question, Why?

5. Change your friends or their mindset.

If I cannot change the mindset of people around me, then I change them. I told you before that the kind of friends you have greatly influences your life. This is one of the best ways to improve yourself. If you cannot change the mindset of the people around you, then you should definitely change them so they don't pull you down with them.

6. Learn a new skill.

If you have one good skill that you are good at, you can never go to bed on an empty stomach unless you choose to, and if you have multiple skills, you can never be broke unless you're lazy. Personally, I have lots of skills, and I'm acquiring more. I can write literally anything; I can speak effectively and eloquently; I can market and sell; I'm a graphic designer; I fix gadgets; and at the time of this writing, I'm learning website design.

Build or improve yourself by learning new skills. Make research on skills that have high demand or will have high demand in a few years to come, and learn one or more so you don't outlive your relevance in the near future.

7. Utilise social media wisely (follow knowledge-based accounts or channels).

This is one of the easiest ways to improve yourself. Social media is accessible to almost everyone, and almost everyone uses it. You can use yours a little differently by using it to improve yourself. Follow social media accounts or channels that offer value, not models or celebrities who frequently post pictures in bikinis. Research accounts that post educational content relating to your chosen career or niche and follow them.

8. Workout or meditate.

Working out helps keep your body in shape, while meditating helps keep your mind in shape. Meditation and exercise can help you improve your mental and physical health, thereby improving your life. There are more opportunities open to fit people than there are to unfit people. Working out gives you a fit body, thereby improving your confidence and increasing the opportunities available to you.

Mental health isn't talked about much, yet ailments associated with it kill faster than other kinds of sickness. One way to retain your sanity and mental health is through meditation. I admonish you to exercise and meditate regularly.

9. Become eloquent

Most of you do not know how many opportunities you can get just by being eloquent; it is a very important quality you must develop, whether you are a man or a woman. A lot of people cannot stand and speak very well in front of seven or eight people. Here is my advice: start cultivating good speaking skills now because very soon you'll become super successful and cannot help but speak to a large number of people; you need to do it very well.

10. Pray.

The powers of prayer are quite underestimated by modern-day Christians. Prayer is one way to access a better and greater version of yourself. You become an extraordinary and powerful person when you are divinely guided. Whether you seek discipline, good health, wealth, or greatness, prayer should be your first option because spirituality controls physicality, and if you can conquer in the spiritual realm, then you will definitely conquer physically.

Every man must seek to become better every day because you become useless and irrelevant when you can no longer improve. Nokia still wishes they had done better.

ACTION STEPS TO TAKE

1. Make getting better at whatever you do and improving in every area of your life your utmost priorities.

2. Find those areas where you are lagging and get better.

FIND PROBLEMS TO SOLVE

A seed cannot maximise its potential if it is not buried in the soil. –
Ezedi Souvenir Isaac

One way to make money is to find a problem to solve, and if you cannot find one, create one. Most of you do not know how banks and insurance companies operate. Do you know that these two industries promote financial insecurity in order for you to use their services?

A bank will tell you the dangerous things that will happen to your life if you do not keep your money with them, and an insurance company will give you reasons why you must insure your properties by creating fear in you. Creating a problem for your customers is a money-making strategy that might not sit well with many people, especially the religious ones.

The Oxford dictionary defines problem as a thing that is difficult to deal with or understand. Now, what happens when you help people deal with something or understand it? They compensate you! Rich people are problem solvers; they either solve problems for fellow rich folks or for the poor. The more problems you solve for people, or the more people you solve problems for, the richer you will become. When you solve problems for people, you're not only making money, but you're also making people like you.

THREE CATEGORIES OF PEOPLE WHO SOLVE THE MOST PROBLEMS

In my life, I have learned and observed that there are three categories of problem solvers, and most inventors and innovators fall into one of these categories.

i. Lazy people

Believe it or not, lazy people are problem solvers because they are always finding ways to make things easier and find easy ways out. I learned this from my mentor, Vusi Thembekwayo. It doesn't always hurt to have a good number of them on your team.

ii. Compassionate people

This group of people is made up of those who care about the wellbeing of others. They always want to see people in better and more comfortable positions. They go out of their way to see that everyone is fine, and from doing this, they begin to become more creative and find ways to make people's lives better.

iii. Naturally smart and creative people

These are the brains behind every idea, either in their workplace, in their lives, or in the lives of people around them. Most of them are born with a high IQ and are naturally creative. They always have a solution to every problem, and even if they don't, give them time and they will figure something out.

SOLVING A PROBLEM

Solving a problem requires you to be humane, compassionate, patient, creative, and persistent. When you develop compassion for humans, you'll always want to see them in a better position and make things easier for them, and from there, innovation is born.

HOW TO SOLVE A PROBLEM

1. Seek to improve people's lives and make them more comfortable.

Innovation is sometimes born out of compassion. If you make making people happy and comfortable your goal, solutions to the problems they face will come to you, and when you can provide a solution to a problem, money constantly visits your bank account.

Always seek to grow your compassion level, intelligence, and ability to create value.

2. Recognise problems affecting you or other people and try to find a solution.

Every product you see solves a problem. Cars solve the problem of transportation, and shoes make sure your feet are protected. Like I always say, the first step in solving a problem is knowing the problem, and the second step is knowing the cause of the problem. To solve a problem, you must first recognise the problem and try to find its source. This problem could be affecting you or the people around you. If you can find a problem and the cause of the problem, finding a solution won't be difficult.

CREATE A PROBLEM IF YOU CAN'T FIND ONE

A lot of religious people may not like this idea of creating a problem if you can't find one and may even consider it dubious and unholy. When I talk of creating a problem if you can't find one, I don't mean you should go out there, hurt people, and offer them a solution. What I simply mean is that you should help people recognise and fully understand their current problem, which they hadn't given much attention to or were completely naive about its existence.

A lady who sells paint went to market her product to a rich man. The man informed her how perfect his painting still looked and why he didn't need the paint. The lady went on to point out the scratches in the walls of the building and scare the man with stories of how his house's painting would fade when the rain came. At the end, the man bought the paint.

The scratches had always been there, and either the man was clueless about them or wasn't paying much attention to them. What the young lady did was simply help the man recognise his existing problems and enlighten him on what would happen if he let the paint slip through his fingers. If you can't find one, you'll be a saviour and a millionaire, maybe even a billionaire.

WHY EVERY MAN WHO DESIRES SUCCESS SHOULD SOLVE A PROBLEM

1. When you solve people's problems, they pay you for life.

One of the ways to create generational wealth is for you to solve a problem, and it is also a good way to make money in your sleep. The inventor, innovator, or someone who comes up with a novel idea might be in his house doing nothing, but the problem he solved is already piling up money for him. You'll become a money magnet when you become a problem solver.

2. It keeps them indebted to you.

I'm very sure the whole world continually appreciates the Wright brothers, who invented the aeroplane, and even Alexander Graham Bell, who invented the telephone. What would we have done without them? Travelling and communication are made easy today because of them. When you solve problems for people, it leaves them indebted to you forever.

In solving a problem, ask for the creator's help. A lot of people might not like this idea, but it is a great way to solve a problem. Ask for the creator's help, and he will be willing to offer it as long as you do everything according to his will. Ask for your creator's help; most times, it is the duty of a manufacturer to maintain a product.

ACTION STEPS TO TAKE

1. Write down the problems affecting you and everyone around you, and write down a possible solution.

2. Write down businesses that have never been started before in your area.

3. When you get an idea, start working immediately.

SAVE LESS, INVEST MORE

If you can recognize and satisfy a demand, you can make money. –
Ezedi Souvenir Isaac

Savings and investments are two things people don't understand, and for this reason, they remain in the shackles of poverty. Savings is the money you set aside for a particular reason, especially to have cash to fall back on, on rainy days, while investments are things you channel into a person's venture, person, or cause, especially to earn returns.

There are three types of investments: investments in a person, investments in a venture or industry, and investments in a cause. There are also three kinds of things that can be invested in to ensure growth. They include time, money, and energy. There's a saying that it's not the amount of money you put into a business that makes it grow, but the time and energy you put into it. This is not completely wrong. Time, money, and energy are needed for the success of a business, and the business cannot thrive very well if some are absent.

Two businessmen have start-up capital of one thousand dollars and ten thousand dollars, respectively. Both spend eight hours daily in their place of business, and both are also running their businesses in commercial and lucrative areas. There's no doubt that the second one has a higher success rate.

INVESTING MISTAKES PEOPLE MAKE

A lot of people don't profit from their investments because:

1. Lack of proper research.

One morning, I was seated with my mom outside our house when she got a call and immediately picked it up. It was my immediate elder sister on the phone. After a while of speaking, she asked my mom to pass the phone to me. Hello," I said, trying to figure out what was so important. She told me she had an update about a paying platform that would help me make money as soon as possible.

Is it the one you've been telling Mummy about? I asked with curiosity evident in my tone. At first, I ignored it, but after some days of trying to convince me, I succumbed. I invested out of pressure and forgot to do my research. The platform crashed, and both I and my sister lost our money. If I had taken time to do research, I would have found out that no one knew the company's founder or CEO and that it wasn't a registered business.

Whatever you choose to do, make sure you do proper research; investment isn't excluded. It is very important to ask questions about the person or organisation you're investing in or investing with. If you cannot do it yourself, find trusted people to help you. If not, get ready to visit the land of failure.

2. Investing because of pressure.

I invested my money in a ponzi scheme because of the pressure mounted on me by my sister. A lot of people have unwillingly or ignorantly invested their money in unsuccessful business ventures because of pressure, mostly from friends or family members. Some invest because people who invest in that particular venture or industry are raking in lots of money. Pressure can make you act without proper reasoning, and eighty percent of people who took decisions without proper thought and consideration failed woefully. Never make investments or investment decisions based on pressure; always endeavour to do research first.

3. Possessing no knowledge of their chosen industries, and not having people who do.

I took a huge risk when I invested in a crypto asset for the first time. I went online, downloaded videos on how to buy cryptocurrency in Nigeria, and went on to purchase cryptocurrency. I had no idea how cryptocurrency worked; all I knew was that it made people rich. A lot of people fall into this category of investors. If you have no idea about your chosen venture or industry, then it is wise that you find someone who does in order to prevent making mistakes that could lead to failure.

4. The urge for quick money or returns.

Your quest for quick success is detrimental to you. A lot of people have gotten themselves involved in illegal things that have ruined their lives as a result of their desire for quick success. It is very good to have a strong desire for success, but it is harmful to have a strong desire for quick success. Never attempt to evade the "you learn and you grow" rule.

There are long-term investments and short-term investments. Most times, long-term investments produce higher returns than their counterparts because they grow over time. Whichever one you choose; you must be patient for your investment to start yielding profits. Your focus should be on improving, but do not rush the process.

5. Investing all their money.

The subtitle of this section of the book is "Save less, invest more. It is quite risky to invest all your money. A lot of ventures have failed, and more will fail in the near future. Invest more, but don't forget to save and spend. Saving gives you cash to fall back on in turbulent times; spending satisfies your needs or wants; and investing grows your money. You must learn how to maintain a balance between these three. Don't just invest your money; spend a little and save the rest. You'll notice that your life will become easier.

TYPES OF INVESTMENTS

1. High-risk investments.

These are types of investments that have high risks but produce high returns. The individual or organisation invests their money, knowing full well that it might fail. They include investments in equity funds, crypto assets, foreign exchange markets (FOREX), etc.

2. Medium- or moderate-risk investments

These are investments that have an average level of risk. The risk rating is neither low nor high. Examples of medium-risk investments include investments in real estate, small businesses, or dividend stocks.

3. Low-risk investments.

Low-risk investments are types of investments that have lower risk rates and lower returns. This kind of investment produces low profits, but the chances of making profits are higher. They include investments in high-yield savings accounts, money market funds, fixed annuities, etc.

FORMS OF INVESTMENT

Investments can take three different forms, which include:

1. Investments in ventures or industries.

This is the kind of investment made in companies, organisations, industries, or businesses. I read the story of a man who was starting a movie production company and approached his uncle to be his first investor. His uncle granted his request and invested in his production company, which he later experienced growth in. The man here invested in the movie industry. This is an example of an investment in a venture or industry. There are other examples, such as investments in stocks.

2. Investments in people.

Some time ago, I was with my immediate elder sister, who was accompanying me to the hospital. She looked into my eyes and said to me, "I know you might be wondering why I'm doing all this for you. Beside the familial ties we share, I'm making an investment in you and want to be part of your success story."

Investments in people are a type of investment where a person or organisation spends their time, energy, or money to ensure the growth or success of another individual or group of people. Parents make investments in their children by sending them to school; this is why it would be a shame for your parents to die poor after investing heavily in you. Just like investments in ventures, investments in people can also fail.

3. Investments in causes.

This is a type of investment whereby an individual or organisation channels their resources towards a cause. I started investing my time and energy in trying to create mental health awareness on social media platforms after dealing with a big emotional problem. This is an example of investing in a cause. This particular type of investment isn't profitable most of the time because it is mostly for charity, but it can help you grow and establish your influence.

BENEFITS OF INVESTMENTS

1. Financial freedom.

The major benefit of investing is to grow your money and become richer. Investments, when made properly, can make you a master of money until the day you transit into the world beyond.

BEST FORM OF INVESTMENT

Cryptocurrency, stocks, and bonds can all rise and fall. Industries can encounter problems, maybe even fold up, and the latest or trending investment opportunities can become obsolete, making earning returns difficult. One thing that will never fail is you; this is why it is absolutely necessary to make investments in yourself. One good way to invest in yourself is to learn multiple skills. The more skills you have, the more valuable you become and the greater your chances of success.

SAVINGS

Pay no attention to those who advise you to save all your money, and ignore those who tell you to invest all your money and not save at all. For you to become successful, you must be able to maintain a balance between savings and investments. Use the "Save less, invest more" rule. Investments may fail at times, and what will you fall back on when they do? This is why it is best to save a percentage of your money, spend a little, and save the rest.

POPULAR MYTHS ABOUT SAVING

There's a kind of boring life most of our parents lived. Go to school, get a job, save a percentage of your salary, and build or buy a house with the money you save. Then retire with some money. The mistake was that society taught them that saving would make them rich. Savings can actually make you rich, but it will definitely take a longer time, and it isn't a sure way to become rich.

Imagine two workers who earn the same amount of money: one saves fifty percent and the other invests thirty percent. There's a higher chance that the one who invests will get rich faster than his colleague. Money has the ability to grow. Your one thousand naira, rands, cedis, dollars, or pounds could make you lots of money when utilised properly. Therefore, saving is good, but investing is better.

Saving Tip: Aside from your normal savings, have another savings account that only you know about and never touch it unless it is absolutely necessary to do so.

Savings and investments are both necessary for exceptional people like you who desire wealth. If you learn how to create a balance between both of them, then your chances of success will be greatly increased.

ACTION STEPS TO TAKE

1. Challenge yourself to save a percentage of what you earn monthly, invest another percentage, and keep the rest.

AVOID OR UTILISE DEBT

Financial literacy is the first step to financial freedom. – Ezedi Souvenir Isaac

Here, you have the option to either avoid debt or utilise it for your own benefits. In plain terms, debt is the sum of money that someone owes. A lot of people don't yet understand that debt can either make you or destroy you. Proper utilisation of debt can make you a millionaire or even a billionaire, and poor use of debt can leave you at the mercies of poverty forever. You must be able to understand debt and how it works in order to use it properly for your own personal gains.

BEFORE YOU BORROW

Before you think of borrowing or taking a loan, ask yourself certain questions. These questions would help you determine whether or not you should be borrowing money in the first place.

1. What am I borrowing for?

Should you be borrowing money in the first place? There are good reasons you should borrow money, and there are bad reasons to borrow. One bad reason to borrow is to spend, and another is to pay off other previous loans. It's totally fine if you're borrowing to invest, but you also need a sufficient amount of knowledge of the industry or venture you are investing in in order to reduce or completely eliminate your chances of failure. You should also have backup plans if you are borrowing to invest, because not all plans work out.

2. Who or where am I borrowing from?

A lot of people have shared their experiences borrowing from loan sharks, whom they became total slaves to. Borrowing from a loan shark can completely ruin your life. These loan sharks can come in the form of people or organisations; they ask you to pay high interest rates for small amounts of money, and by doing this, they convert you to total slaves. You work, and they earn.

Also, if you are borrowing from friends or family members, make sure they are patient and kind people. Don't borrow from greedy people, people with trust or anger issues, or people who will try to take advantage of you or your situation. There have been many cases of parents who gave their daughters away in marriage because of their inability to repay a loan.

3. How do I pay it back?

After loan and loan utilisation comes repayment, how do you pay it back? Or are you going to let your integrity and self-respect go down the drain because of your inability to repay a loan? Money has a very powerful influence on those who let it; it has ruined the strongest and most solid relationships, and you will be surprised at how a long-time friend will immediately change towards you when you're unable to repay the money they lent you.

Make proper plans before taking a loan, and how you will pay it back should be inclusive. If you don't have any solid way to repay the loan, then you should consider forgetting about it. The answers you get from these three questions will determine if you are going to borrow or not.

PROPER UTILISATION OF DEBT

In the book The Richest Man in Babylon by George S. Classon, a certain man who received fifty gold coins as a gift from the king as a result of his hard work came to ask a money lender for advice because his sister was requesting he loan the money to her husband. One of the pieces of advice that the money lender gave him was that he should ask his sister's husband what he needed the money for before lending it to him.

If death is used properly, then you may never have to borrow again. The problem is that most people don't know how to utilise debt, or they borrow for the wrong reasons. The best way to get the most out of debt is to borrow to invest. Invest in yourself or in something that will bring returns.

Most of the successful men you see started out with loans because you will rarely find people who will give you money for business start-ups. Most people want to see that your business has become successful before they can invest in you or your enterprise because they are trying to ensure the safety of their money. We learned in the previous parts of this book that there are three types of investments. The ones I will strongly advise anyone who wants to take a loan to make are self-investment and venture investment.

The best form of investment to make is in yourself, because everything may come and go, but you'll always be there, and you'll always be able to make money for yourself. Also, if you are investing in industries or ventures, ensure that you have a sufficient amount of knowledge about what you're investing in or have someone who does. Endeavour to know more about your investments, even if you have people who do.

DO YOUR OWN RESEARCH

Whether you are investing in yourself or in a venture, research and plan. Researching will help you figure out a lot of things, such as whether the organisation is a scam. Who are my co-investors? Does this industry or venture have the ability or resources to grow? Etc.

WHERE TO FIND LOANS

This is a problem most people have, especially those who live in Africa or underdeveloped countries. This particular job is left for you alone to do because only you truly know your financial capabilities, so you should be the one to do the research. My advice is that whatever person or organisation you choose to borrow from, make sure they are trusted, their interest rates are favourable to you, and you'll be able to repay.

ACTION STEPS TO TAKE

1. Whether or not you are going to take a loan doesn't matter, but if you do, make sure you take a loan and do the right thing with it. The right thing is to invest.

LIVE BELOW YOUR MEANS

Wealth comes to those who learn how to create wealth and implement wealth creation methods. – Ezedi Souvenir Isaac

You should be able to endure a few years of pain for a lifetime of pleasure. You'll only be scared by the "live below your means" rule if you have not set definite goals for your life with plans on how to achieve them. Buying luxurious, fancy, or expensive things is good, but it is mandatory to live below your means while on your growth journey.

Most youths begin to develop financial problems and indulge themselves in crime when they try to live above their means. Time is very powerful; it can bring anything. If you think smart and grind hard, then there's no doubt you'll definitely become successful one day. Most times, our greed and desire to live above our means are born out of the expensive lifestyle we see rich people live.

The funny thing is that even rich people live below their means because if they didn't, they would go broke. Before a wealthy person spends a hundred thousand dollars on a car, he has definitely made more. Another category of people who unknowingly or unintentionally promote greed are social media influencers. It is safe to say that most live a fake life, and others are able to afford such luxury because they are sponsored by brands.

During my early days in affiliate marketing, I was making a decent amount of money but couldn't afford nice clothes. My family assumed I was being stingy, and my mom doubted I would be able to take care of my family in the near future, but they just didn't understand. I had dreams of purchasing things better than the latest jeans or Nike sneakers. I wanted lifelong financial freedom, and temporal pleasures were the sacrifice I had to make for permanent pleasures.

Dele had just gotten a new job at one of the private firms in the city. It had been his lifelong dream to get a job in order to escape poverty. In his mind, he thought he would be in a much better financial situation if he could get a job. Dele was surprised he was still suffering after getting a job; he began to think his salary wasn't enough and went back to doing menial jobs on weekends.

One day, he came across a podcast video where the anchor said, "You will never grow financially if you have hoses connected to you that waste all your accumulated resources. After listening to this podcast, Dele decided to take some time to meditate. He realised that his girlfriend, Cynthia, had the nicest clothes, shoes, and gadgets, and her bank account was never devoid of cash, and he was the one who made this possible. She was the biggest hose, tapping about 90 percent of his resources. Dele loved her too much, but he realised she had to go for him to grow, and eventually he broke up with her.

Some of us are still fighting financial battles because of certain people or things in our lives—things we think we cannot do without. There are some people and things you have to let go of before you can grow and become successful.

HOW TO LIVE BELOW YOUR MEANS

A lot of people struggle to live below their means, and it has crippled them financially. Here are a few steps to living below your means:

1. Always remember that there are always going to be nice things.

My mum used to say the world was never going to run out of nice things. Knowing this will help you establish a certain kind of financial discipline and conquer unnecessary wants. Some time ago, Blackberry phones were regarded as a sign of wealth or luxury, and those who didn't have this phone were seen as low or middle class.

At the time of this writing, the cell phone world is dominated by iPhones and Samsung. It's foolish to stress over the latest or nicest things because there will always be better. Have this at the back of your mind, and it will help you curb unnecessary spending and live below your means.

2. Look at your temporal wants and your permanent wants. Compare them and determine which you want more and which you should sacrifice to get the other.

Are you willing to sacrifice getting a Lamborghini in the near future for the latest model of an iPhone? This is what you will be doing when you succumb to purchasing or spending on expensive things that are way beyond your financial capacity during your growth journey. You should be able to make a sacrifice for the greater good. Grant Cardone once said, Pay the price today so you can pay any price tomorrow. Think of what you really want to achieve and where you want to be, then compare them with what you currently want.

3. Learn budgeting.

Budgeting is an important financial skill to learn, especially if you are a young person. Having good budgeting skills can decrease your chances of encountering financial challenges, even if you do not have much. Receiving an income is one thing, but utilising your income so it benefits you is another. A lot of people suffer because they lack financial management skills like budgeting. There are lots of people who live a good life with a meagre salary or income; this is because they know how to budget and put their money to good use.

THE BENEFITS THAT ACCOMPANY LIVING BELOW YOUR MEANS

I got some advice from my junior secondary school English teacher that I'll never forget. She said, "When you have a cob of corn, don't eat it. Plant it and go hungry for the year because you'll certainly have an abundance of corn in the next year—more to eat and more to sell. This means two things: sacrificing and investing. We sacrifice and invest for the same reason: for blessings or for the greater good. A short time of pain for a long time of happiness

Everything you are purchasing should have the ability to make you money or grow your money. Unnecessary spending or living above your means can leave you broke or even poor if you don't control it.

ACTION STEPS TO TAKE

1. Cut out unnecessary spending and live below your means.

2. Do not get into debt if you cannot use it.

GROW IN SILENCE

Before something can grow, it must first be born. Start first and grow later. – Ezedi Souvenir Isaac

Mr. Joe stepped out of his newly acquired Mercedes Benz and walked into his father's compound. The large crowd gathered there, staring and murmuring in shock and disbelief. Joe, the cheap labourer, was now a wealthy person. He had instructed his workers to share gifts with the villagers since it was Christmas.

Joe was one of the poorest and least respected men in the community. He was over thirty but still lived in his father's house. He had asked several girls out, and they turned him down instantly, saying they didn't want to associate with a poor man like him. He had attempted suicide several times, but the constant appearance of a bright sun in his dreams kept him motivated.

For several months, he had been working so hard to improve his life. At the beginning of the year, he vowed he would never end the year the same way he began it. He disappeared for some time and dedicated his time and money and energy into achieving his goal. No one, not even his family, knew where he was or what he was doing. He just kept calling to assure them he was fine. Now the trash had become a treasure.

Growing is good, but growing in silence is better. There are billions of people in the world, and I think all of them will be happy to see you succeed. Unpredictability and discreetness are two weapons you can use to conquer your enemies.

HOW TO GROW IN SILENCE

1. Don't share your growth journey unless you have to.

Unless you are a celebrity, an influencer, or some social media personality, sharing your growth journey isn't really necessary. It's better to leave them confused and shock people with the results. I realised that if I told people my plans somehow, it would be unsuccessful, so I began to keep them to myself and maybe a few trusted family members. Everyone knows I'm doing something, but nobody knows what.

2. Do things to improve your life daily and speak to no one about them.

The principle of aggregate marginal gain states that if you decide to improve on a particular skill by as little as 1% every single day, you will be better than at least 90% of people who have that skill.

BENEFITS OF GROWING SILENCE

1. It gives you fewer enemies and helps you conquer your existing ones.

Before we can master an enemy, we must know its name, habits, and place of abode. Your enemies destroy you because they know too much about you. My body always reacted to snacks that were fried with oil, and I opened up to a friend of mine. One day, while we were having a conversation, she told me that she didn't need poison if she wanted to harm me. She just needed to feed me fried pastries in my sleep.

Your enemies become more powerful when they know you, and you also become stronger when you know your enemies. That is why moles were sent to infiltrate opponent's dwellings during wars in ancient times. You must keep them in the dark and conquer them with the power of secrecy, because what people know they kill, but what they don't know or understand they talk about.

2. It makes your growth sweeter.

There's a magical feeling you get when people who have previously seen or regarded you as ordinary see or notice that you've grown or become better. Growth is sweeter when people are completely clueless about how you grow. It is better to grind in silence and let your success make the noise.

3. It makes you unpredictable and powerful.

Unpredictability is one of the greatest sources of power. If you live in an area where no one wants to see others grow, unpredictability and secrecy can help you win. Growing in silence makes you a powerful person.

4. It helps you achieve your goals faster.

Growing silently enables you to avoid naysayers, and naysayers slow down the achievement of your goals. When your enemies cannot stop you, they slow you down. Being quiet about your growth will enable you to learn, grow, and improve at a faster rate. For some people, when you keep speaking to people about achieving your goals without actually achieving them, your brain could start deceiving you into actually believing you have achieved them, and you become intoxicated with a non-existent success.

You become more powerful when you become unpredictable. Complicated people are respected and feared the most because not much is known about them. People are completely clueless about their strengths and weaknesses. If you incorporate this technique into your career, you will become invincible.

ACTION STEP TO TAKE

1. Make people completely oblivious to what you're doing to improve your life. By so doing, your success will be unexpected and shocking.

BE WILLING TO MAKE SACRIFICES

Most times, much is needed to achieve much. – Ezedi Souvenir Isaac

Everything you do in life requires sacrifice, but not all sacrifices are good. No matter the money-making route you take, you will be required to make sacrifices. It could be your time, hard work, dedication, fun time, or even your relationship with people. Not all sacrifices are good, and not all sacrifices are accepted societally.

Back in secondary school, I had a biology teacher who we called Mr. Tofa. He was so smart and brilliant that this man never brought a note or textbook to class. He had everything in his head, including diagrammatic illustrations. The most amazing thing was that he had more than one class at that time. Thrilled by his intelligence, I walked up to him after class one day and said to him, Sir, I'm impressed with how you are able to teach without any aid like a text or notebook. How were you able to achieve this?"

He laughed and said to me, "When others were playing ball, having fun, and doing irrelevant things,

I was busy studying. I usually woke up at midnight to study, and after the rain, I would attempt to draw and label diagrams on the wet floor. I thanked him for his advice, but the first question I asked myself that day after he left was, "Am I really ready to make such a sacrifice to attain what he did?"

Sacrifices are necessary for the actualization of goals and the achievement of dreams. The greater the sacrifice, the greater the blessing. In the Bible, Abel was favoured by God because his sacrifice was greater than Cain's. Solomon sacrificed 22,000 oxen and 120,000 sheep; this was why he was richly blessed. Every successful person you see has made a sacrifice.

An example is Grant Cardone, who sacrificed fun for success, and another is Gary Vaynerchuk, who sacrificed personal pleasures. Martin Luther King, Jr., knew better when he said, "Human progress is neither automatic nor inevitable. Every step towards the goal of justice requires sacrifice, suffering, and struggle—the tireless exertions and passionate concerns of dedicated individuals.

WHY EVERY MAN MUST SACRIFICE

Sacrifice is very necessary if a man is to grow and become successful. Every successful person got to where they are through sacrifice; some might be smaller than the rest, but all are considered sacrifices.

1. It helps you grow.

Sometime ago, I began to learn about social media marketing and script writing. I lived in a noisy environment; my house was close to the main road, and my room was close to my mom's shop, which was regularly filled with customers. It was almost impossible to learn in those days. I bought courses, and the only time I could use them was at night.

I sacrificed my sleep and rest because I wanted to be better. Sometimes I was even tired from the day's work, but I always woke up at night because there was something I wanted to achieve. At the end of the story, I became very good at the two things I sacrificed my time, sleep, and energy for. If you are not willing to make sacrifices, then your chances of attaining growth are impossible.

2. It destroys mediocrity.

Consistency and persistence are two weapons that can turn mediocrity into exceptionality. These two powerful tools are a form of sacrifice that people make to attain success or greatness. Being consistent or even persistent hurts and is not always easy, but everyone must evade mediocrity. People have overcome mediocrity and become great versions of themselves because they made sacrifices during their growth journey.

3. It creates a better future for you.

In the Bible, Solomon never fought a battle, but David did. David made all the sacrifices so Solomon could be free. Your sacrifices may hurt presently, but they will definitely create a better life for you in the near future. Some of the battles and things you endure are short-term, but they will create a lifetime of financial freedom for you.

4. It gives you long-term success.

Sacrifice enables you to enjoy long-term success. Depending on the gravity of the sacrifice Great sacrifices enable you to enjoy long-term success. If you want to establish yourself, enjoy lifelong success, or give those around you a better life, you must be willing to make sacrifices.

5. It helps you become disciplined.

Sacrifice requires you to drop certain acts like drinking alcohol, smoking, gambling, and womanising, which will in turn help you become disciplined. Grant Cardone revealed that he had to quit playing golf in order to focus on his goals. Even discipline is another form of sacrifice, and discipline is developed through sacrifice.

6. Sacrifices place you as a model for others.

The crowd cheered as a young lady, probably in her mid-twenties, walked up to the podium. Her smiles were captivating, and the young men began drooling over her. A young black woman graduating as the best student at a foreign university. Everyone was wondering how she was able to achieve such a great feat. According to the young lady, it had always been her dream to be the best graduating student, and she had sacrificed her fun time with friends, her sleep, and even her money.

TYPES OF SACRIFICES

There are two types of sacrifices: acceptable and unacceptable. The acceptable is a type of sacrifice that is accepted societally, and the unacceptable is the complete opposite of the acceptable. In Abeokuta, Nigeria, four men were charged with the murder of a twenty-year-old lady. The perpetrators of the crime killed the young lady and burned her head for ritual purposes. This is definitely a sacrifice, but an unacceptable one. Any good sacrifice should bring physical pain to you and not to others.

SACRIFICING

There are three categories of sacrificants: those who don't know the sacrifice to make; those who know the sacrifice to make but are finding it difficult to make because it is difficult and instead embrace mediocrity because it's easier and safer; and those who make the wrong sacrifices to get quick wealth. Money, time, energy, happiness, love, patience, friendships, or relationships are some of the things that can be sacrificed.

The law of sacrifice states that the greater the sacrifice, the greater the blessing or reward. Everything you desire in life requires you to make sacrifices, and financial freedom is no exception. Some things require smaller sacrifices, while others require larger ones.

ACTION STEP TO TAKE

1. Write down the things you want clearly on a piece of paper, and write down what you are willing to sacrifice to achieve them. For example, "I want to be a super social media influencer, and I'm willing to sacrifice my time, energy, and money to achieve my goals."

DO THINGS DIFFERENTLY

*Madness is simply seeing something from a different and abnormal
perspective. – Ezedi Souvenir Isaac*

At one time, everyone was going through the stress of finding publishers for their books until someone decided to access a hidden part of their brain and do things a little bit differently. This is why e-books are common today. Just because everybody else is doing something in a certain way doesn't mean you should too. There are billions of things in the universe one can try out, and there are numerous opportunities you can seize for yourself.

WHY YOU MUST ENDEAVOUR TO BE DIFFERENT

Why do one thing over and over again when there are numerous things to try out? Only a mad person does the same thing over and over again and expects a different result. Most times, you can only achieve a better result when you start thinking or doing things differently. The major reason you must endeavour to be different is so you can get better results.

FOUR RULES OF BEING DIFFERENT

I formulated four rules every man should follow if he endeavours to rise above average, become different, and change his life. These rules will help you attain exceptionality.

1. Think differently.

Elon Musk is a human just like you; he has the same brains you do and the same bodily features you have. The only difference between Elon Musk and an average person is that Elon thinks differently. To conquer certain problems, you just have to think differently.

i. Think of ways to improve your life.

The first and most important way to think differently is to think of ways to improve your life. This particular type of thinking is the most powerful among all, and if you give enough time to it, you'll become a much better person than you can ever imagine. The first step to becoming better is to realise you were created for more; the second is trying to figure out how to achieve more; the third is implementing the ways of achieving more that you have thought out or learned; and the final one is achieving more. While simpletons think of stupid and irrelevant things, an extraordinary person like you should be thinking of ways to better your life.

ii. Don't think of problems; think of solutions.

The average person thinks of and dwells on his problems, but the exceptional one tries to find solutions to his problems. The challenge is that the world is filled with people who have embraced mediocrity.

One day, I realised something that greatly changed my life: if you sit down and continue thinking about a problem, there's a chance that the same problem will be present the next day and the day after, and you would have just wasted your precious time. Instead of overthinking a problem and drawing insanity to yourself, think up a solution. Approach each problem with the intention of solving it, and a solution will come forth.

iii. Filter your mind and evacuate negativity.

This is another step towards thinking differently. Our mind is like a bucket; it can hold whatever you put in it, whether solid or liquid. We unknowingly fill our minds with negativity, either because of the things we watch or listen to or because of the people around us. You can hardly achieve anything tangible with a dirty mind because it will always hinder you. Look at yourself and try to determine which parts of your mind are negative and filter them out.

2. Act different

Action comes after thoughts. The second level of achieving something is action. If you are serious about achieving your goals, you must change your actions. Your actions determine whether you earn money or not; this is why your actions are very important. If you act the right way or do the right thing, you could be a millionaire in a short while.

i. Change what you watch

Our eyes are the most important sense. Most of our daily activities are aided by our eyes, which is why a deaf or dumb person can live a normal life and a blind person can't. We collect information with our eyes and retain it in our brains. What we see or watch greatly affects our lives, which is why those who are addicted to porn view the opposite gender lustfully. The eye feeds information to the brain. A lot of motivational speakers tell people not to sit around in front of a television, or else they will be poor. I believe this is untrue; everything has the potential to change your life positively or negatively; it depends on how well you utilise it.

A lot of people have committed suicide because their naked pictures were leaked on social media, and at the same time, a lot of people have made lots of money from social media. If you must watch television, then whatever you're watching must be able to change your life positively, or else you're just helping someone else become richer and more famous at the expense of your time.

ii. Change what you read.

A lot of successful people tell us that they read their way out of poverty and ignorance, and we believe it, but trust me, they didn't achieve this with romance or erotica novels. Often times, I hear people say what you read doesn't matter; what you do with what you read does, but there's little you can do with a romance novel, so what you read also matters. Change your genre of books to self-help, and you will be a better person in no time.

iii. Change your daily routine

What you do every day either brings you closer to achieving your goals or pushes you farther them. Every day, endeavour to take actions that will place you in a better position in less than one year. Examine your life and detect the things you do on a daily basis that have zero benefit to your life, and change them immediately. It could be watching irrelevant content, eating junk food, gossiping, or even scrolling through social media. Change your daily routine, and your life will change greatly and positively.

iv. Relate with like-minded or intellectually superior people.

My mum used to say that if a person seeks wisdom, the easiest way to attain it is to move with older people. I countered her by saying that foolish people also grow old, and then I realised that one can learn from a person's wisdom as well as their foolishness. The easiest way to become wise is to move with wise people, and the easiest way to become rich is to move with rich people. If you want to become successful, then you must change the kind of people you relate to because they'll certainly affect your behaviour.

When government or research facilities want to achieve a goal quicker, they bring a group of scientists together not just because of their knowledge but also because they want to push each other to their limits, thereby speeding up the goal achievement process. Relate with like-minded and intellectually superior individuals, or relate with the kind of people you want to become.

3. Talk Differently.

A lot of people can speak hundreds of words a day, but none are inspiring or educational, while others cannot even hold proper conversations. Our words hold great power, and we can create or destroy things or people with them. The majority of people have died from depression that sprang up from what people said to them or what they said to themselves.

If you grew up in an African home, then the sentence "there is power in our tongue" shouldn't be new to you. As children, we were admonished to affirm positive things in our lives, and my mom would never fail to scold or hit you when you said negative things to yourself.

i. Speak positively, especially to yourself.

There is no magic or supernatural power attached to optimism; it works in a simple and natural way. When we speak things to ourselves, our minds receive the information and use it when giving instructions to others.

The body is a servant of the mind. If you say something positive constantly, your mind begins to receive the information regularly and begins to steer your body in the direction of making that thing a success. When you wake up every morning, speak positive things to yourself so your mind and body can grow into believing and achieving them. This also works any time of the day.

ii. Engage in meaningful conversations.

I heard a quote from someone one day. Avoid any conversation that you cannot learn from or that does not make you laugh. If you desire success, separate yourself from the 90 percent of people who are bent on saying nonsense. Discuss ideas, dreams, and educational things. Don't discuss people unless they are successful; discuss ways to be like them or to be better; don't criticise or ridicule them.

4. Eat Different.

A lot of people are experiencing challenges in their health and life in general because of their poor eating habits or diets. People pay less attention to what they eat because they feel it is unimportant, and Nigerians will tell you that the stomach cannot disclose what comes into it. What they don't understand is that what you take into your system is one of the determinants of how healthy you will be. If you eat rubbish, then your health will be rubbish.

i. Drink water regularly.

The health benefits of water are too numerous to mention, but one of them is that it boosts skin health and beauty. One of the biggest sources of the inferiority complex is the belief that you are physically unattractive. Water helps your skin look healthy, thereby boosting your confidence and your ability to attract people.

Unpopular Fact: Physically attractive people are more open to opportunities than their counterparts.

ii. Avoid junk food.

Replace junk foods with healthy home-cooked meals, and you'll be grateful you did. The biggest negative effect of eating junk food is that it causes obesity, which messes with your self-confidence and other important areas of your life. People look at you and automatically think you're incapable of handling an important task just because of the way you look. It can reduce the opportunities available to you and decrease your chances of earning.

The Hard Truth: The reason obese people don't think of becoming better is because people around them tell them they are beautiful the way they are. Here's the hard truth: you can achieve little if you're obese, so get up and work on your life because your creator never built you to be an object of ridicule.

iii. Avoid alcohol and drugs.

I avoid alcohol at all costs because I want to retain my speed-thinking and problem-solving abilities. Drugs may give you excitement and confidence, but they're only temporary; every hard drug has its own disadvantages. Marijuana increases one's chances of developing breathing problems or cardiovascular diseases; heroin messes with your brain; and cocaine causes malnutrition, gastrointestinal issues, kidney damage, and liver damage. Addiction to drugs or alcohol can also affect your ability to save and invest. Avoid alcohol and drugs if you crave success.

MY PERSONAL CHEAT CODES FOR BEING DIFFERENT

i. I trained my mind to always see opportunities, even when and where there are problems.

Sometime ago, a lady who lived close to us was relocating to a new city. She couldn't bring all her properties along with her, so she decided to sell some of her items, including her dog. She approached my mum with the intention of selling the dog; my mom and sisters were seeing a pet while I was seeing an investment.

My intentions were to buy the dog and purchase a male dog so they could procreate and I could sell their children. The idea was quite funny and ridiculous, but at the time, it was very unorthodox. Billionaires don't think like average people; that's why they are billionaires.

In every problem, there is always an opportunity; it's just that some of us haven't trained our minds to see it yet. The majority of the world's inventions were developed because of various problems. Always try to find opportunities in problems; this doesn't mean you should exploit other people's weaknesses.

ii. I use envy and jealousy to my advantage.

The difference between a regular person and an extraordinary person is not just how they think but also how they act when faced with problems. Jealousy can be a very powerful tool if you use it wisely. Some of the big things I achieved were because I was envious of people who had achieved them before me.

I believe the creator built the emotions of anger, love, hatred, jealousy, etc. to steer us in the right direction when used properly. When mediocre people are jealous of certain people, they criticise and mock them, hate on them, or even work towards harming them or causing their downfall, but when exceptional people are jealous, they work towards improving themselves or becoming better than the people they are jealous of.

iii. I find new ways to do things.

The problem with most people is that when something does not work for them, they start believing that it was never meant to work. Everything is meant to work for you, but not every method. For example, everyone has the potential to become successful, but not everyone can become successful through the entertainment industry.

There was a story of a young prince whose father disliked him because he was bad at using a sword. The king had an empire and needed his sons to become good soldiers in order to help him hold it. The young prince's elder brothers were already training to become good swordsmen, and they all mocked him for it.

One day, he relocated with his mother to his maternal kingdom. There, he met new people and began training again. He realised that he wasn't good at using a sword but was a beast with a spear. The same thing happens in our schools. No student is dumb; it's just that every student has their own learning methods and triggers, but teachers don't understand this, and those who do, do not have time to analyse the students and discover their individual learning methods.

I always find new, easy, and creative ways to do things, and when I do, I always emerge as the best. This is one of my superpowers. There are more than one million ways you can become a millionaire. Find three or more that you can do very well and believe can work for you. Start with one and keep the rest as backup plans.

The universe was built and filled with different opportunities and options, some of which we haven't discovered yet, but all for our benefit. There are so many things to try in order to achieve success. When you make the decision to be different or do things differently, people will consider you boring or abnormal, but not to worry; you are the one who's going to be chilling in the back of a Rolls Royce, not them.

ACTION STEPS TO TAKE

1. Train your mind to recognise opportunities and to see opportunity in every difficulty.

2. Become a visionary and think ahead of anyone; it doesn't matter if they call you weird.

REPEL NEGATIVITY

If you can tolerate any kind of behaviour from people, then, you'll go far in life. – Ezedi Souvenir Isaac

Our mind becomes like a trash can when it is filled with negativity. Negativity can be the result of the words of naysayers and critics. To become successful, you must learn to handle these two things. There are billions of people on the planet, and though it is possible to please them all, it is the most difficult task.

Negativity is an attitude that is not hopeful or enthusiastic. No one should subject their mind to negativity because what you ingest into your mind controls your reasoning, and your reasoning controls your action.

GUIDELINES FOR REPELLING NEGATIVITY

1. Learn to deal with mockery and rejection.

Just forget about success if you're not ready to deal with mockery. Most people do not understand the role mockery and rejection play in the life of a man who is hungry for success. Mockery is the act of mocking, ridiculing, or degrading. Mockery is usually initiated by people with no foresight or those with bad judgement skills. The truth is that you should never take mockery from those you wouldn't go to for advice.

2. Shun naysayers.

There are people who exist just to criticise and oppose people in the most unreasonable way. These people are mostly simpletons, or they are just jealous of you and are feeling insecure for a particular reason. Pay no attention to naysayers because nothing positive comes out of them. You must learn to ignore them and repel every form of negativity they emit.

If you are in Africa, there's a possibility that you are surrounded by archaic people, those with low IQs, or people who don't want to see you grow. The best thing to do is to ignore them.

3. Learn to deal with critics or bad reviews.

The best way to deal with criticism is to build on it. I told you that problems come to break us, but we can use them as stepping stones to greatness. Some of the things people criticise or give bad reviews on actually have a problem. In fact, you should be happy that someone was able to see the flaw in your product or whatever and call it out immediately. Reassess your product, notice the flaw, and improve it immediately.

4. Practice optimism and feed your mind with positivity.

I began by telling you that what you ingest into your mind controls your reasoning, which in turn controls your action. A study has proven that people who watch porn have a lust-filled mindset. Feeding your mind with negativity exposes you to depression and other mental health problems, which will hinder your success. Feed your mind with positivity at all times. This is a great way to repel negativity.

5. Surround yourself with positive-minded people.

The people around you or the people you associate with have a huge influence on your life. You are the sum total of the five people you regularly spend your time with. There are people around whom success becomes difficult, and there are others who make failure difficult. The best people you can be around are optimistic people, because when situations get tough, they'll act as pillars and help you hold your life together. Problems are inevitable, but with the right people and strategies, you can overcome them.

6. Meditate.

Meditation has so many benefits and has proven effective in all areas of life. Meditation opens your mind to new ideas and enables the quick solving of a problem; it is also necessary if you must maintain your sanity. Sometimes, all it takes to rid your mind of the excess negativity that has accumulated over time is to practice meditation.

NEGATIVITY AND THE HUMAN MIND

Here are reasons you must protect your mind and repel negativity at all costs:

1. Repelling negativity helps you retain your sanity.

You'll be more mentally stable and at peace when you start to repel negativity. Most times, mental problems result from something in your mind that shouldn't be there. Warding off negativity is good for your mental health and will help you find clarity in whatever you choose to do in life.

2. It improves your creativity and productivity.

You become more creative and productive when your mind is at ease, and one of the ways to develop a calm mind is to repel negativity. It is difficult to think properly and access the exceptional version of yourself if your mind is filled with filth. A wild person with a calm heart can do anything, and ideas are constantly present in calm minds.

3. It helps you win.

Repelling negativity makes you more productive and creative, which in turn helps you become successful. Sometimes, to win, you just have to filter your mind and extract its pessimistic contents. When you begin to repel negativity, your focus will improve, thereby increasing your creativity and productivity and enabling you to achieve more.

4. It helps remove unwanted people from your life.

Repelling negativity includes repelling its sources, the naysayers! There are people you will need to grow with, and there are people who must be as far away from you as possible if you are to elevate in life. Whoever does not support your goals or does not want to see you improve should not be part of your life, no matter who they are. Repelling negativity will help you extract these types of people from your life.

5. It makes you a better person in terms of character and a better judge of character.

Our minds find It is difficult to make good decisions or judgements when the air is polluted. A lawyer whose client was a victim of rape appeared before court with the sole intention of making sure the accused was persecuted. This woman fought aggressively to see to it that the young man was sent to prison.

The victim didn't have much evidence and was drunk the night she was raped; she only accused the young man because he had asked her for a dance in the club that very night she was raped, which she refused. The evidence wasn't solid enough, and it was obvious the boy wasn't guilty, yet this lawyer fought ferociously. The truth was that the lawyer was raped as a child and hadn't healed properly.

It's not always difficult to notice someone who's been hurt terribly in the past or someone whose negativity dominates their life. Most bullies you see were either bullied or are feeling insecure. You will be able to see people for what they are rather than what they are not and develop a good attitude when you rid yourself of negativity. All the ugliness you see in people is only a reflection of your own true nature.

Overall, it is absolutely necessary to free your mind of negativity if you are to grow and become successful.

Negativity restrains us from living up to our maximum capacity, keeps us from achieving more, and instils the feeling that we are not good enough in our minds.

ACTIONS TO TAKE

1. Avoid friends or people who criticise ideas, dreams, visions, or goals, and surround yourself with people who make failure difficult.

2. Recognise the areas where negativity rules in your mind and free your mind of negativity.

BE HUMBLE

Everything around us has the ability to make or break us. – Ezedi Souvenir Isaac

One trick you can use to get anything you want from people is to respect them. Every man wants to be honoured and accorded respect, despite his age, size, background, social status, or economic status. You will be surprised at how much you can achieve through humility.

Poverty can be a result of either stupidity, laziness, or pride. A lot of broke people are narcissists; they are too proud to accept they are naive and to ask for help. When I don't know something, I endeavour to ask a question, regardless of who I ask, as long as you know what I want to learn.

The Cambridge Dictionary defines humility as the feeling or attitude that you have no special importance that makes you better than others; lack of pride. Confucius was right when he said that "humility is the solid foundation of all virtues."

The problem with some poor people is that someone who knows more than they do or has achieved more than they have will try to teach or help them, and they'll endlessly express their stupidity and naivety, thinking it's knowledge.

One painful thing in life is being naive or ignorant without having any idea you are, because if you have a problem and you know you have a problem, you know how to seek a solution. The first step in solving a problem is knowing the problem, and the second is determining the cause. Dana Arcuri said that "true humility is staying teachable no matter how much you already know."

WHY SHOULD ALL MEN BE HUMBLE?

1. A humble man will have several opportunities to learn, but a proud man won't.

This one works best for those who are in their salad days. If you're young, one good way to learn is to be humble. Never act as though you're more intelligent or knowledgeable than everyone around you. For example, if you are learning a skill under the tutorship or mentorship of a teacher or coach, be modest and learn.

2. A humble man will grow; a proud man will be constrained.

The Bible states that pride comes before a fall. Humility creates an atmosphere for you to grow. One fact is that when humans (whether poor or rich) are respected, they feel a certain kind of obligation towards you and are moved to help you.

Automatically, they are compelled to favour you in any way they can. It could be by rendering financial help, recommending you when opportunities arrive, or offering assistance when needed. Crush your ego to dust if you desire growth. Also, do the same if you have already grown or are in the process of growing. This is mandatory for whoever wants to remain at the top.

3. A humble man will be open to numerous opportunities; an arrogant man won't and will find favour before men.

My sister's brother-in-law rose and became a multimillionaire without doing much. One day, he parked his old, rickety vehicle and headed into the market in Victoria Island, Lagos. While walking, a man who was in the area that particular day called him. The man was very specific and made it known that he wanted to speak to him in particular when the other man beside him replied. He went closer to the man and said to him, "I've been seeing you around, and I've noticed how humble and respectful you are. I want you to come and manage my properties.

The man had multiple real estate investments and put my sister's husband and brother-in-law in charge of them, all because of humility. Most people, including world leaders, pick humble men to rule alongside them because they want to be sure you won't try to challenge their authority or give orders that counter theirs. Most people like people they can control, make them feel in power, and get whatever they want from them.

4. Humility can improve your relationships with people.

Growing up, I was a little proud, and it affected me until I decided to change. I grew up with older people, and I was better at relating to older people than my age mates. I felt like everyone around me lacked knowledge, so I isolated myself from them. It began to cause problems for me, even with my teachers. At that time in school, I had only two friends because they were the only ones who were willing to listen to and understand me. I began to change in senior high school. I still didn't relate much to people, but I was better, and one more person was added to my circle.

No one likes arrogant people; even God Almighty detests them.

5. It improves your relationship with God.

If you are a Christian, then you should already know by now that God detests proud or arrogant people, and you should be aware of the story of Lucifer and the fallen angels. Humility helps you attract favour and help, whether solicited or not, from God, just like you would from men. God is always happy to render help to us whenever we ask in humility. Humility can improve your relationship with God and men. For a Christian, humility is indispensable. Without it, there can be no self-knowledge, no repentance, no faith, and no salvation.

HOW TO PRACTICE HUMILITY

1. Practice gratitude.

Pride can develop when you start to believe that people owe you more or that you deserve worship and admiration from them. In simple terms, humility means respecting all men, regardless of who they are. True gratitude is being thankful for the little things we have, not the huge things. Learn to show gratitude to men and to your creator, no matter what. Even if you buy something from a merchant with your money, say thank you to them. It screams humility.

2. Listen to and tolerate others, despite who they are.

No matter how foolish and ignorant someone is or sounds, it's important to listen to them so you don't become like them. We make decisions on what we want to be and do by taking surveys and studying everything available to us, then moving on to weigh the pros and cons. By hearing the bad and the good, you decide which you want to do. Humility demands that you listen to and tolerate all men, in spite of their age, financial status, or personality.

3. Respect everyone, irrespective of their social or economic status.

In this life, there are those who honour the rich and disrespect the poor, and there are those who honour neither the rich nor the poor, and these people are mostly poor people. You should be able to see beyond people's economic and social status and accord them the respect they deserve. This doesn't mean you must associate with them or give them your full attention.

4. Solicit help whenever you need it.

Humility is accepting that you cannot do something and showing a willingness to learn. We were never born to be flawless, but we were created with the ability to learn, improve, and grow. Pride makes you intoxicated with your self-worth and strips you of your ability to learn, tampering with your potential to improve. If ever you need help, go to those who are capable of rendering it to you and ask nicely.

5. Admit your mistakes and be open to correction.

The proud men are women who foolishly believe that they are flawless and beyond correction. Every man is prone to mistakes, and what we owe ourselves is to learn from them and become better. Sometimes we offend people or do wrong things without realising it, but we should be able to admit our mistakes when we realise them and seek ways to make amends.

6. Extract the idea that you're better than everyone else and be open to correction.

This kills potential faster than anything else. Anything that is perfect is dead. You lose the willingness and ability to improve or become better when you start to believe you are better than everyone else. This is the tool pride and arrogance have used in destroying potential, ending many lives, and reducing great men or intending great men to zero. Beware of this dangerous tool; filter your mind and extract the belief that you are better than everyone else so you can regularly improve and access concealed and better versions of yourself.

7. Obey the laws guiding you, whichever place you are.

Most often, disobedience to the law is a result of believing that the law isn't accurate or that we are above the law. You must instil in your mind that no matter who you are, you are not above the law, and obedience to the law is mandatory. Humility requires that you obey the law in whichever place you find yourself. Not only does this give you a good reputation, but it also helps you thrive even in foreign lands.

THE MAN WHOSE HUMANITY WAS RAISED

There is a story of three friends: one a lumberer, the other a petty merchant, and the last a fisherman. These three friends were very poor and could barely feed their families; they had no knowledge or connections to make money except for an old friend who was extremely wealthy.

One day, the petty merchant, considered the poorest and most ignorant yet the most ambitious, came up with a proposal. He said, "Let us go to our old friend and ask him not for monetary but for intellectual help on how to make money. Immediately, one started laughing, and the other shunned him.

The fisherman said to him, "How can we go to our old time friend with whom we started life together to ask for help? What does he know that we don't, and what is so special about him? The second one said, "Have you no shame? How do you think his wife, children, and slaves will take you when they see you asking for help from him? If you must go, then go alone."

Disappointed, the man decided to embark on the journey alone. The next morning, he prepared and visited the man. He got to the man's house and was informed that the man wasn't home. So he came back at noon and met the man. The rich man was happy to see his old lumberjack friend and offered him a drink and some exotic meals, but he refused and told him that he didn't come for that.

He narrated to his friend how he had been in the shackles of poverty and his strong desire to break free. He simply admitted he needed help. His friend smiled and told him that wasn't a big deal and he should come back the next day. He left happily and came back the next day. The man told him that he would help him under the condition that he would work with his apprentices, and he accepted. The rich man's intentions were for his friend to learn the basics of making money.

A few months later, the poor and ignorant lumberer became very wealthy; his success was considered one that came overnight. His friends were still plagued by poverty, and out of jealousy, they began to attribute his success to luck.

Humility can raise low and average men into power, and it can raise powerful men to become more powerful. If you truly and strongly desire success, you must not downplay the power of humility. Most people are afraid to be humble because they believe humility is associated with weakness and that they will lose respect. According to C.S. Lewis, humility is not thinking less of yourself but thinking yourself less. You can be humble and still maintain your self-confidence and exceptionality.

ACTION STEPS TO TAKE

1. Learn to respect and honour people, no matter who they are or where they come from.

2. Practice humility, but know when you're being too humble.

PRIORITISE INTEGRITY

The beauty of integrity cannot be fully explained words. – Ezedi Souvenir Isaac

The day was in its early hours when three men rode on two separate bikes and arrived at a compound. Their facial expressions were a mixture of happiness and worry as they hopped down from their bikes.

Are you sure he will succumb? You know he is a tough and stubborn man," the tallest one among them said, putting on a serious face. "He will when he hears the amount we are offering," the other said. "I agree with Chukwuka," the shortest one replied with so much confidence as he pulled the key from the keyhole of his motorcycle.

They advanced towards the entrance of the house and banged on the door. A middle-aged woman wearing an oversized shirt, visibly displaying her nipples, with a wrapper on her waist and a scarf on her head, walked out. She greeted them and inquired about who they were and what their mission was.

Madam, we just want to see Eze; is he around? The shortest one asked She looked at them, confused, and summoned the courage to speak again. "Any problem?" She said. No, we just have an opportunity that will favour him; he's a long-time friend." The shortest one spoke again.

After mentioning that they had an opportunity for him and that he was their long-time friend, the woman began to loosen up and trust them a bit. Her serious face brightened up. She informed them that her husband had gone to check his traps on the farm to see if they had caught any animals. They decided to wait, and the woman offered them seats. A few minutes later, Eze, a man who was in his early fifties, walked in majestically with a wrapper on his waist and a chewing stick hanging in between his lips.

Immediately after they saw him, they began to chant his name and praise him in a sycophantic way. He met them and greeted them because he knew two of them. They returned his greeting and asked him to sit, saying that they had something important to say that would favour him greatly.

Eze, we know you are a man of integrity, but this thing is not favouring you. You have to go out of your way a little bit so you don't die of poverty. You're a man, and your wife needs to be taken care of, or else infidelity comes into your marriage. We have a proposal; the governor has approved the project we wrote to him about the other day, but we have planned to intercept the money when it comes and direct it to our purse. But we will need your signature, so we want you in on this. The short one spoke, smiling dubiously.

Emeka, may my ancestors strike me dead if I ever partake in such activity. You plan on stealing government money? This is the height of it! He yelled.

How many times has the government stolen our money? Do we complain? James, the tallest one, said it, and his friends agreed.

Emeka, if you don't take these rats and leave my house, I'll go inside, bring my gun, and make sure I shoot you all," he yelled.

Eze, we can work things out; aren't you tired of poverty? Emeka said, trying to change his mind.

"Get out! You petty thieves Mind you, if anything happens to that money, I'll write a petition to the governor myself and expose you," he thundered.

His wife came out after hearing the loud noise, but as a typical Igbo man, he authoritatively instructed her to go in as it was the business of men. The men left

Eze's compound disappointed that very day, and the project's money was saved from kleptomaniac fingers.

Integrity is a virtue every man must possess. Sometimes it doesn't pay to be a person of integrity, but the character alone is beautiful. Integrity is the quality of being honest and having strong moral principles. This is one of the characters you should develop on your journey to success. There's a quote from Tom Hanson that reads, "Creating a culture of integrity and accountability not only improves effectiveness, it also generates a respectful, enjoyable, and life-giving setting in which to work."

INTEGRITY AND ITS BENEFIT TO MAN

A lot of people will argue that men of integrity rarely profit from it these days, but I can assure you that they do. Society hardly comes across such men, so they appreciate them whenever they do and endeavour to honour them. If you belong to races like African, Latino, or Asian, then you should make achieving integrity one of your goals because it speeds up your success, especially if you live in the western world.

1. It brings honour and respect.

Men of integrity will always be respected, no matter what. Low-class men have been singled out and awarded or rewarded because of their integrity. Integrity brings honour and respect, and honour and respect give you a good reputation. Having a good reputation increases the number of opportunities available to you, which then increases your ability to earn and become successful. This is the circle.

2. Integrity opens doors to opportunities.

Even those who scam, steal, or deceive people like having people they can trust around them. There's an old African saying that those who use machete on people never allow others to use it on them. Integrity can create opportunities and open doors for you because people need people they can trust.

3. It presents you as a role model for society.

A man who had never dreamed of being on television in his life was interviewed one day. According to the man, he had grown up in a family where poverty was lording over them, and that same poverty was still present in his life. This man was a petty trader to whom a customer wired more money than she was supposed to.

The interesting thing was that the man lived in a totally different city from the woman, and she couldn't even recall where his shop was located. Yet he made his way to her town to refund her the additional money. For a long time, this man was a model to everyone, and those who were capable did everything in their power to honour him.

To do good, you must first know what is bad, discern between the two, and choose the one you want to practice. Whenever you're torn between choosing integrity or dishonesty, ask yourself, how do I want to be remembered when I'm gone?

4. It gives you a sense of fulfilment.

There's a certain kind of pride I get whenever I resist evil. Acting or taking decisions based on integrity gives you a sense of fulfilment. You'll feel like you have conquered a particular enemy or won a certain battle.

HOW TO DEVELOP INTEGRITY

Here are some simple steps to develop integrity and positively change your life:

1. Learn the act of gratitude.

Being grateful for what we have helps us develop integrity. Being thankful doesn't mean we should accept our situation and not seek to improve it; it simply means that we should be thankful for what we have rather than lamenting about the things we don't. The art of gratification can repel so many negative and immoral things from us and help us develop discipline.

2. Develop honesty.

There is no integrity without honesty. Honesty is the foundation on which integrity is built. Truthfulness is a virtue and will help develop trust. One good thing about being honest that I've found out is that even when you decide to be dishonest, everyone still trusts and believes you, even though the trust can be broken if you're eventually caught. If you desire success, endeavour to be truthful at all times.

When approaching investors, tell them the truth about your idea, your business, the revenue it has generated, and how their money will be invested. Saying the truth doesn't necessarily mean you can't withhold certain information to prevent your intellectual property from being stolen.

Honesty attracts a certain calibre of people to you—men and women of high standards. It opens you up to opportunities because successful people like having people they can trust around them, not people who exist to flatter or milk them.

3. Sincerely or faithfully serve your God and honour your religion.

Faithfulness and sincerity towards one's religion or God can help you develop integrity.

Some treasurers in a church planned to commit theft and informed their colleague, trying to get him to join them. The man refused, saying his religious beliefs and his faith in God would never allow him to do such a thing. Same with a Muslim who refuses to drink alcohol because his religion forbids it. Our religion and belief in God or our creator can prevent us from engaging in lots of dirty or immoral acts and help us develop integrity.

4. Keep your promises.

One way to become a man or woman of integrity is to keep your word. It doesn't show responsibility when you make promises to people and don't fulfil them. It reduces you to an average person and can negatively affect your business life. One reason most people will buy from you is because they know you on a personal level or are convinced they can trust you.

In business, one thing you should try to establish is trust, and you can do this by keeping your promises. Always do something whenever and however you say you will. If for some reason you can't, give an explanation to your customers, apologise to them, and endeavour to make it up to them.

5. Strive to make money, but never become a slave to money.

Money is an important factor in our existence, and we should all strive to make money. But we lose our integrity and become slaves to money when we let money control us. The majority of the crimes people commit and some of the terrible things that happened were the result of an excessive taste for money. You need a strong desire to be rich, but you also need to develop strong moral principles so you do not become a beast in your process of acquiring wealth.

Integrity can place you above your peers in business, your career, or society in general. The beauty of integrity cannot be fully explained in words.

ACTION STEPS TO TAKE

1. If you are a businessperson or are in any other field, use integrity to establish your brand, retain your customers or audience, and gain new customers or audiences. Make your brand reputable in such a way that no one can doubt whatever comes from you or your brand.

2. Be more sincere in your dealings with people. Wealth acquired illegally doesn't last.

READ REGULARLY

Sometimes, you never get answers because you ask the wrong questions.
– Ezedi Souvenir Isaac

Women who read are dangerous, but men who read are powerful. I developed the stiff neck theory after I realised that all the people around me who disliked reading were naive and foolish. Reading opens our minds and expands our brains. The creator built us with a special kind of intelligence that can be accessed through constant learning, and one of the greatest ways to learn is by reading.

Every phone is built with a certain storage capacity that cannot be exceeded, but our brains can learn billions and even trillions of things without being exhausted. The power of the mind should never be underestimated.

THE STIFF NECK THEORY

The stiff neck theory, formulated by me, simply states that an ignorant man is like a man with a stiff neck; he can only see what's in front of him, but when he begins to open up his mind to learning new things, his neck begins to turn and he begins to see things from other corners.

BENEFITS OF READING

1. It increases your knowledge.

A man who reads and a man who doesn't can never be at the same level in terms of knowledge. This is because we access converted or unknown information when we read. Reading is like an exercise or workout for the brain. The law of reading states that the more you read, the more you know. Personally, self-help books are what I recommend, but I strongly advise that you read anything that has the ability to change your life positively.

2. It changes your mind (positively or negatively).

Every book is a reflection of the author's perspective. By reading, we are able to expand our horizons and see things from a different perspective, which will aid us in making better judgements and inferences. A book can either change your mind positively or negatively. There was a story I read one day about a Christian guy who came across a book about angels and demons. He stated that halfway into the book, his mindset began to change, and he tuned into believing

God was at fault for unjustly throwing Satan and his demons down to earth.

Books played a huge role in shaping my mindset about money and life in general. The right books can change your mindset positively, and the wrong books can do something entirely different to your mind. Read books, but be extremely careful about the kind of books you read.

3. Reading changes how we view the world and improves our understanding of how it works.

One of the best books I've ever read is Think and Grow Rich by Napoleon Hill. In the book, I discovered the powers of thoughts and how to transform them into their physical equivalents. I learned how to apply philosophy to several aspects of life. The more you read, the more your perception of life changes, and the better you understand how things work.

4. Reading improves your writing abilities.

This is not just exclusive to writers or authors. Writing dominates almost every part of our lives. Musical artists write their songs before performing them; scripts are written before movies are acted; and even writing is done in the office. Reading helps us become better writers because, when we read, our brains automatically and subconsciously copy the author's style of writing. Most times, we are not even aware this is happening.

5. You can become motivated or inspired simply by reading books.

I once read a memoir that told the story of an African girl and her experiences in love, relationships, and her career. The funny thing was that I was coincidentally experiencing some of the emotional challenges she wrote about at that time. Humans are fragile creatures and can be broken emotionally and physically. Knowing that someone had experienced the same thing I was currently experiencing inspired me and motivated me not to give up. This is how powerful and life-changing an act as simple as reading can be at times.

6. It is a form of therapy for some people, e.g., me.

When I'm angry or sad, I write to empty my mind of the junk accumulated over time, and I read to empower my mind in order to see beyond my current emotions. While this might not work for everyone, it is still very helpful. Often times, one can find solitude and clarity in books.

7. It improves your speaking

I learned something from Vusi Thembekwayo; he said that one way to become better at public speaking is to have full knowledge about what you want to talk about. Reading helps you speak without errors, and by reading, you receive sufficient information on various contents that will ameliorate your speaking skills. Most public speakers don't know everything about the subject they talk about, but when they are given a topic, they start doing research immediately, master the given topic, and present their speech effortlessly and flawlessly.

8. It improves communication and interaction skills.

So many people cannot communicate effectively, especially in the presence of knowledgeable people. Most people have nothing to contribute to a meaningful discussion other than "seriously," "really," "okay," "that's great," "you don't mean it," etc. One day, I was in the midst of a group of men, and they began a conversation about the early Catholic Church.

I wasn't even a Catholic, but I contributed meaningful and knowledge-impacting things to their discussion, so they began to ask, what school do you attend? The misconception was that every brilliant child attends a good private school. Reading enhances your communication and interaction skills, thereby improving your relationships with people.

9. It improves your vocabulary.

At a very young age, I had a very good vocabulary. This was not because I was taught in school, but because of the books I read. I could remember vividly; I was nine then. My mom and I were visiting my aunt in a city close to my hometown called Asaba. We were in a bus, and the window was faulty; it couldn't slide. I was close to my mom, who was beside the window.

I became hot and was attempting to open the window, but my efforts were fruitless. Then I said, "Mummy, I'm getting claustrophobic. That day, everyone in the bus was very shocked. A lot of people don't make efforts to learn new words. Often times, they display their ignorance and naivety and end up embarrassing themselves.

10. Reading can make you rich if you read the right books and implement what you have learned.

This statement comes with a condition. It means that you can only become rich if you read the right books and implement the things you've learned. Reading is one thing, and practicing or implementing what you've learned from the books you've read is another. Knowledge is potential; it only becomes power when applied effectively. This simply means that what you know doesn't matter; what you do with what you know does. When I read books or learn new things, I endeavour to practicalize them no matter what, or else I've just wasted my time.

BEST BOOKS TO READ

1. Think and Grow Rich, by Napoleon Hill

This book comes first on my list because it is my best. If you want to become successful, this is one of the books you must read. It was originally published in, and personally, it was one of the first I read. Napoleon Hill scribbled down the secrets to success in this book; he explained how to transform thoughts into their physical equivalent.

2. Maximising Your Potential by Myles Munroe

This is another book I love so much. The author explains how we can fully unlock and utilise our God-given potential. He also stated that we should endeavour to die empty, not old. This simply translates to dying after living a fulfilled life.

3. Rich Dad, Poor Dad by Robert Kiyosaki

Robert Kiyosaki is one man you should listen to his teachings if you plan on becoming rich. He teaches people how to evade taxes. In his book, Rich Dad, Poor Dad, he stated that the rich don't work for money; they make money work for them.

4. Success Through a Positive Mental Attitude by Napoleon Hills and W. Clement Stone

This is another book by Napoleon Hill that I also love. It was co-written by W. Clement Stone. In this book, he explains how to achieve success through optimism and the use of a philosophy called Positive Mental Attitude (PMA).

5. Knockout Entrepreneur by George Foreman

This is a book every entrepreneur, salesman, or woman should read. The book was written by a former well-known boxer named George Foreman and Ken Abraham. He taught and explained how he applied the techniques of boxing in business and how effective they were. From this book, I learned that champions in business are not born; they are made.

6. The Richest Man in Babylon, by George S. Clason

While scavenging through my brother-in-law's book shelf, I found this book, and I'm grateful I did. Here the author reveals the money-making strategies of the ancient Babylonians. He tells the story of three poor men who decided to go to their old friend, who was the richest man in Babylon at that time, and ask him how he acquired riches.

7. As a Man Thinketh by James Allen

I got this one as an audiobook on my phone, and I always enjoyed listening to it, especially when I'm taking an afternoon nap so it can sink and sit in my subconscious mind. In this book, the author highlights the powers of thoughts and how to utilise them effectively in order to achieve success and greatness.

8. The Science of Getting Rich, by Wallace D. Wattles

I also got this one as an audiobook from an app on my phone. It highlights the importance of adding value to others and explains how to create wealth using simple methods.

9. The 10X Rule by Grant Cardone

Grant Cardone's story is one that inspires me—how he rose from being a drug addict into being one of the most successful salesmen. This is a must-read for every entrepreneur or whoever is in the sales business.

10. Start From Where You Are by Praise George

This one was written by a Nigerian author and book publisher called Praise George. In this book, I learned the power of small beginnings. I was highly inspired to start whatever I wanted to do at that time. This is one of the books that have greatly influenced my life.

11. Atomic Habits: An Easy and Proven Way to Build Good Habits and Break Bad Ones, by James Clear

This is a comprehensive guide on how to get better every day by simply changing your habits. The author clearly states the power of small habits and how they can make a big difference.

12. The Seven Habits of Highly Effective People by Steven Covey

Steven Covey, an American writer, penned down the seven habits of successful people. The first is proactivity, and the last is sharpen the saw, which means to constantly work on improving yourself.

Originally published in 1989, the principles can still be applied in modern times.

13. How to Win Friends and Influence People, by Dale Carnegie

This is a self-help book, and its content isn't far-fetched from the title. It basically talks about how to make people like you and make the most out of friendships or relationships using simple and common techniques. If you're in business or any other form of career that requires human relations, try out this book.

14. Vusi: Business and Life Lessons from a Black Dragon by Vusi Thembekwayo

Vusi Thembekwayo is one of my favourite people on the internet. I follow him on every social media platform he's on, and I get a notification whenever he posts a video on YouTube. He's a man filled with wisdom and knowledge, and his eloquence allows him to effortlessly impart knowledge to those who listen to him. Vusi: Business and Life Lessons From a Black Dragon is one book I recommend for every entrepreneur.

15. You Are a Badass: How to Stop Doubting Your Greatness and Start Living an Awesome Life by Jen Sincero

I love this book because I hate mediocrity and everything associated with it. I believe no one should accept ordinariness because our creator had better plans for us while building us. If you want to level up in your life and maximise your potential or God-given talent, then this book is definitely for you.

16. Young Black Millionaire: How to Rise Above the Limitations of Age, Colour, and Race to Become Successful by Ezedi Souvenir Isaac

This last one is the very book you're reading now, written by a young African boy. Here I've penned down simple ways to succeed at that work, no matter your age, race, the career you choose, or the background you come from. I have made it clear that mediocrity shouldn't be our only option because we come from a particular race or live in a particular area. Keep reading, and I can assure you that you're just one step away from success.

Reading is a very important factor for our growth, and though society may favour rich men, educated men still have spots in the hearts of the people. The more you read, the more things you will know. The more things you know; the more places you will go. Sometimes, how far you go isn't determined by the people you know but by how much you know.

ACTION STEPS TO TAKE

1. When you finish reading this book, write down all the lessons you have learned and occasionally make time to study them.

2. Challenge yourself to read at least five other books in areas like business and finance, character development, motivation or inspiration, and history.

BE DISCIPLINED

A man isn't truly respected by the kind of money he has but the kind of value he offers and the class he exhibits. – Ezedi Souvenir Isaac

I don't think Bill Gates or Mark Zuckerberg watch porn. To be successful, one must learn to maintain discipline around alcohol, the opposite gender, and even money. Discipline is another beautiful quality one can have; it simply means having self-control and knowing when to say no to certain things.

Discipline can sometimes be determined by the things you do when no one is watching, not what you do before multiple eyes. Some time ago, I came across pornographic content while viewing a friend's WhatsApp status. No one was watching me, and I was alone. I could have stayed behind and continued watching the video, but I didn't; I skipped it with immediate effect.

Discipline pays, no matter how boring it may look or how ugly and displeasing the ignorant people around you may try to make it look. It is one of the sacrifices you need to make in order to achieve wealth or greatness. You must learn how to live life like the monks while on your journey to success.

HOW TO BECOME DISCIPLINED

1. Know when to say NO.

A lot of people have a problem saying the word no, and that is why they encounter challenges most of the time. The word no is composed of two letters, yet it is very powerful. Knowing how to say no to certain things like drugs, alcohol, sex, women, and other things you don't need will help you develop discipline and become a better person in life.

2. Quit pornography; it hasn't and will never help you.

It's very foolish to watch people do what you want. Porn has never helped anyone except the actors who make money from it or the crew who are part of the filming process. It is one of the major reasons many youths have not been able to achieve tangible things or hit major milestones in their lives. The effects of pornography on individuals include:

i. Lustful mindset

Pornography turns you into an animal. It changes your mindset and makes you see the opposite genders as toys for sexual satisfaction. A relationship where a partner is addicted to pornography cannot last because, odds are, there will be no communication, emotional interaction, or even true feelings. It's just going to be sex all the time.

ii. Distraction from goals

If most people who are addicted to pornography spent the time they spent watching this erotic content trying to achieve their goals, some of them would have been successful by now. If the Devil cannot stop you, he slows you down, and pornography is one of the tools he uses to achieve his dubious goals. If you spend your time and energy on pornography, it will be extremely difficult and almost impossible for you to be successful.

iii. Temporary disconnection from God.

I'm not sure that there's any religion in the world that supports sexual immorality. If you're a Christian, pornography can disconnect you from God and make you derail from the track to heaven.

3. Avoid Masturbation.

Masturbation is the twin brother of porn; they work together, and addiction to porn can lead to masturbation and other forms of sexual immorality. Masturbation refers to the fiddling of one's private organs to gain sexual pleasure. Masturbation is one of the things that can slow down the achievement of one's goal. If the devil cannot stop you, he uses certain things like porn, masturbation, and family problems to distract you. This is why you must learn and cultivate discipline.

4. Quit alcohol.

All the mistakes I've ever made in my life have been when I've been drunk. I haven't made hardly any mistakes sober, ever. Tracey Emin. Every disciplined man must be able to say no to alcohol, even if he gets criticised for doing that. It is one of the criteria for becoming disciplined.

5. Know when to speak and when to shut up.

A disciplined man knows when, where, and how (tone and language) to speak. Most people who lack discipline try to talk and defend opinions or ideas in places they aren't even supposed to speak. For example, I have little to no contribution to any conversation that is solely based on vulgarity. Before you think of contributing to that discussion next time, ask yourself, Am I even supposed to be here, or do I really have anything to say to these people?

6. Know where to be and when to be there.

Before going to a place, ask yourself, Am I supposed to be there? If the answer is yes, then ask yourself, at what time am I supposed to be there? There are places where you should not be seen or found as a disciplined person. While working on your goal, there are several places you need to avoid; one of them is a bar.

7. Always keep your promises.

When I speak of keeping your promises, I don't just mean the ones you make to others but also the ones you make to yourself. It is dishonourable to break the promises you make to people and foolish to break the promises you make to yourself. Breaking promises is a result of indiscipline. I want you to look around, and you'll notice that the undisciplined people around you don't keep their promises. For example, a man starts dating a girl and promises her that he will not touch her until their wedding night, but because of his lack of discipline, he begins to make sexual advances towards her, thereby breaking his promises.

8. Practice your religion faithfully and serve your God sincerely, not hypocritically.

This is one big way to be disciplined. No matter which religion you practice, honour your God and serve him faithfully. It helps you set boundaries. For example, a Muslim knows he shouldn't drink alcohol because it is against his religious beliefs, and it has helped him set boundaries.

WHY YOU SHOULD BE DISCIPLINED

1. Becoming disciplined is very necessary because it is an attractive quality.

Most people may not understand how beautiful the act of discipline is. Everyone loves disciplined people, even though some may try to keep it hidden. Even if you're not yet rich, the quality of discipline is enough for the moment and would make a great tale for the younger generation. I'm sure it will be prestigious to tell your children how you shunned indiscipline in a society where it dominates.

2. It makes you focus on your goals, thereby speeding up their achievement.

If you can learn to say no to alcohol, sex, porn, masturbation, distractions from gadgets, and the opposite gender, then you've cultivated the quality of self-control and conquered yourself. The greatest form of victory is conquering yourself. Learning to say no to certain vices will help you develop discipline and channel all your productive force into the generation and implementation of your ideas, the achievement of your goals, and the realisation of your dreams.

3. It attracts the right kind of people to you.

A disciplined man will attract disciplined people to himself. This is because people love to move with like-minded people, so they can always have someone who understands them and can put them back on track if they begin to get derailed. Most ladies haven't noticed that the way they dress determines the kind of men they'll attract. If you wear clothes revealing your cleavage, there is a higher chance that you will attract young boys or perverts, but if you dress in a disciplined manner, you will attract responsible men.

4. It gives you a good reputation.

A good name is said to be better than riches. People may mock you because you don't smoke, womanise, or take alcohol, but trust me, when an opportunity arises and a responsible man is needed to undertake a particular task, you'll be the first person they turn to. This is because you have established a good reputation through discipline.

5. It can decrease your chances of developing health problems.

Health problems can be one of the greatest constraints to growth and progress. I'm a living witness. It is difficult to maximise your potential if you are sick. Some health challenges can be the result of indiscipline. For example, a prostitute can contract STIs as a result of her personal indiscipline, and a smoker may suffer from lung cancer. Discipline helps to keep our actions in check, thereby reducing our risks of developing certain health issues.

ENEMIES TO PERSONAL GROWTH AND PROGRESS

1. Alcohol.

I was scrolling through social media one day when I saw an artwork that was used to illustrate the dangers of alcohol. A hand was holding a bottle up in a drinking position, and the bottle was sucking the man's face into it. This illustration simply translates to "First the man takes the drink, then the drink takes the man. Alcohol is one of the biggest enemies of a man's personal growth. Many good men have committed different kinds of atrocities while under the influence of alcohol. The effects of alcohol on a man's life include

i. Alcohol addiction can affect your financial life.

It will be very difficult for a man who drinks a lot to save or invest. I lived close to firefighters while growing up; my mom sold drinks at that time. There was this particular firefighter who would come to my mom's shop and purchase multiple alcoholic drinks.

ii. It affects your marital life.

Alcohol intake can wreck your marital life and cause a rift in your household. Many marriages have ended because of a partner's excessive love for alcohol. My uncle's wife would regularly beat him, just like a man would beat his wife, because alcohol had destroyed his life. Before he died, there was no strength left in him. Alcohol is a foe that disguises itself as a friend.

iii. It affects your health.

I had an uncle, my father's younger brother (stepfather), who invested his time, energy, and money into drinking alcohol. He had no preferences; he could take whisky, vodka, or even beer. He enjoyed any liquid that had alcoholic properties. My dad was much older than him, but my dad looked way younger than him. His alcoholic nature was inspired by my paternal grandfather; in the end, my uncle died earlier than he should have.

iv. It affects your mental health.

Alcohol kills your brain cells and reduces your thinking capability, thereby affecting your decision-making and problem-solving abilities. While under the influence of alcohol, a man loses his ability to think productively and come up with solutions for certain problems, and if alcohol use persists, he can develop a severe mental problem.

THE LIES PEOPLE TELL THEMSELVES ABOUT ALCOHOL

1. A lot of people resort to alcohol as a result of sadness or depression. Some of them are like, "Drinking helps me forget my sorrows. When I have a problem, I try to find solutions rather than trying to

avoid it, because after running, I will come back, and the odds are that the problem will still be there.

Alcohol is just like music; it may give you excitement, but I can bet everything that I've got that it's only temporal. My brother-in-law once told me that meditation is the eye of the spirit. There's no problem without a solution. If you have a problem, meditate and try to think of solutions rather than drinking.

2. The opposite gender.

A lot of men cannot control themselves before women, and likewise, some women. So many men have been reduced to zero as a result of their love for multiple women. Distraction or loss of focus can be a result of obsession with the opposite gender. It could also result in lust. It is understandable that a man needs a woman, and a woman needs a man. Find a person who will help you grow or support your growth, and stick with them and remain faithful to them.

3. Porn and Lust

Anyone who is hungry for success should endeavour to run away from porn and lust, no matter what. Dreams, ideas, and potential are dying on a daily basis because of these two things. Time that could have been spent on the achievement of goals and the realisation of dreams is spent viewing explicit contents that have zero benefits to the consumer. If we continue to watch porn, then we might end up with a society dominated by lecherous individuals.

4. Televisions, phones, and other mobile devices (in some cases)

Being different demands that you do things differently. A lot of people have become millionaires just by using their phones differently than others. Phones, televisions, and mobile devices are great sources of distraction. A lot of people give so much time and attention to these things that they forget to work on their dreams, goals, or ideas.

One tip that helped me stay focused was creating a schedule. I developed my own personal timetable, and by doing so, I was able to create time for work and pleasure. I didn't rid myself of fun and, at the same time, worked hard. Another tip was to follow the right people on social media and watch the right content.

My news feed was filled with posts from entrepreneurs, motivational accounts, crypto traders, forex traders, news platforms, car manufacturing companies, wristwatch manufacturing industries, and the aviation industry.

5. Friends (in some cases)

I said friends can be enemies to personal growth and progress, not bad friends. Friends can, knowingly or unknowingly, become constraints on your personal growth. Assuming you bought a course on a particular skill, you take out your laptop and attempt to watch this course, and a friend comes by and complains about how you've become a workaholic lately. Then she offers to take you to a party. After much persuasion, you reluctantly agree.

Now, this friend has good intentions, which are to make you enjoy yourself at the expense of achieving your goals. For him or her, he has done the right thing. Use my change your friends or change your friends rule to attain discipline and implement positive changes in your life. It simply means changing your friends and replacing them with new and better people if you cannot change their character or behaviour.

The truth is that being disciplined is difficult and boring, but it is part of the sacrifices you must make in order to be successful and enjoy lifelong financial freedom. If you are a person who lacks discipline, there's still time to make changes and make your life better. Take a survey. You can ask yourself or the people around you about the sources of your indiscipline. If you find the source of the problem, then finding a solution will be a piece of cake.

I admonish everyone (young or old), but especially the young ones who are hungry for a better life, to become more disciplined and develop self-control. If you do this, then you might be on your way to riches. A house isn't built in a day, but progress is made every day until the house is completed and ready to become a home. This could be your first step towards achieving your goals.

ACTION STEPS TO TAKE

1. Stay away from alcohol, women, and sex until you have achieved your goals.

2. Quit pornography and masturbation if you are already addicted to them.

3. Endeavour to achieve every goal or carry out every task at the beginning of the day. Don't procrastinate.

4. Know when to say no, especially to certain things that have the capability to ruin your life.

HAVE FUN

There comes a time in our life where dilemma kicks in and everything doesn't feel right but it is left for us to fix ourselves. – Ezedi Souvenir Isaac

---

Once in a while, make time to do something fun or something that makes you happy. Life is nothing without fun. In order to live a happy and fulfilled life, we must make sure our lives are filled with as many fun memories as possible. Life is too short to stress all the time. Make it your goal to make your life fun.

One good thing is that having fun re-energises you for work. Some might say that fun distracts you; well, it only distracts when you try to do it over and over again without restrictions and control. Spoil yourself, my dear phenomenal and exceptional people; you've got one life, and you only live once.

Life is a precious gift, and it's up to us to make the most of it. In the midst of all our ambitions, dreams, and hard work, we must never forget the importance of having fun. After all, what's the point of achieving success if you don't take the time to enjoy it? In this chapter, we'll explore why having fun is not just a luxury but a necessity for living a happy and fulfilling life.

THE JOY OF FUN

Imagine a life where every moment is filled with joy, laughter, and excitement. That's the life we should all aspire to create for ourselves. Fun is like a magic elixir that rejuvenates our spirits, recharges our energy, and reminds us of the beauty of living. It's the spice that makes the journey of life truly worthwhile.

Think about the times when you've laughed so hard that your stomach hurt, or when you've experienced the thrill of doing something adventurous. Those moments are like gems in the treasure chest of life. They remind us of our humanity, our capacity for happiness, and our need for spontaneity.

BALANCING FUN AND RESPONSIBILITY

Some might argue that fun can be a distraction, taking us away from our responsibilities and goals. But that's only true when fun becomes an obsession, when we indulge without limits or restraint. Like everything in life, balance is key.

Imagine you're a chef creating a delicious dish. Each ingredient adds its own unique flavour to the final product. In the same way, fun is an essential ingredient in the recipe for life. When used in moderation, it enhances our overall experience. It re-energises us, sharpens our focus, and makes us more creative and productive.

THINGS YOU CAN DO FOR FUN

1. Explore Nature

Take a hike in a nearby forest, go camping under the stars, or simply have a picnic in the park. Nature has a way of grounding us and filling our hearts with joy.

2. Pursue a Hobby

Whether it's painting, dancing, playing a musical instrument, or gardening, hobbies are a fantastic way to unwind and let your creative juices flow.

3. Connect with loved ones

Spend quality time with family and friends. Organise a game night, cook a meal together, or have a heart-to-heart conversation.

4. Travel and Adventure

Plan a weekend getaway or a road trip to explore new places. Adventures create lasting memories and broaden your horizons.

5. Volunteer and Give Back

Helping others and making a positive impact on the community can be incredibly rewarding and fun.

6. Celebrate Achievements

Don't forget to celebrate your successes, no matter how small. Treat yourself to something special when you reach a milestone. Life is a fleeting journey, and we only get one shot at it. So, why not make it an extraordinary one? It's essential to embrace the philosophy that "you only live once" and use that as a driving force to make your life fun, meaningful, and memorable.

In the pursuit of success and wealth, always remember to prioritise your happiness. As young black millionaires, you have the power to shape your destiny. Let that journey be a thrilling adventure, filled with fun, laughter, and joy. After all, success is truly sweet when it's accompanied by a well-lived life. So, make it your goal to infuse your life with fun. Create memories that will warm your heart for years to come. Your journey to becoming a young black millionaire should be one of both ambition and enjoyment. Embrace the fun, and let it fuel your path to greatness.

ACTION STEPS TO TAKE

1. Take a little money from your savings and go to a restaurant. Give yourself the best treatment. Go to a spa or any other fun and relaxing place, and make sure you have fun to the maximum.

2. At the end of the day, "tell yourself, this is an example of what I'll be enjoying if I can work hard and be successful." Trust me, you will be motivated to work harder.

QUOTES FROM EZEDI SOUVENIR ISAAC THAT WILL HELP YOU LEVEL UP IN YOUR LIFE

1. Every one of us has something that was given to us by God to make us stand out. Some of us just haven't discovered ours yet.

2. Wisdom is knowing what to do or say in every situation and making sure it's done well so it benefits those around you.

3. You can know the definition of something but not the meaning.

4. The most beautiful things come from the toughest conditions.

5. Two different entities live in us, both speaking at the same time but saying different things. The one that dominates is the one we listen to.

6. I like to express myself on paper because it won't mock, laugh, or even pity me. It just alleviates my pain.

7. Wisdom starts with asking questions and extends to showing gratitude.

8. Instead of pestering people by telling them you built a house, build the house to a high standard and let it speak for itself. High-quality products can market themselves.

9. Sometimes what people do to you is not as painful as knowing they are the ones who did it to you.

10. Bad things don't only happen to good people; they happen to everyone, but we notice them more in good people.

11. Don't force people to know or recognise you; let your success do that for you.

12. Every book you read is a reflection of the author's perspective.

13. None of us was created to be normal, which is why the creator gave our minds the ability to stretch limitlessly.

14. Poverty and ignorance are two things that can limit a man.

15. The journey to wealth is not an easy one, no matter the route you take.

16. You can thrive in places you hate or are hated if you channel the hate into your productivity.

17. Your mind can do great things, but you limit it.

18. There are businesses that thrive in a particular area, time, or season.

19. Everyone is acting somehow because of something.

20. Kill the boy in you and let a man be born.

21. The blacksmith breaks the things he intends to reshape. When God wants to make men, he breaks them.

22. Men who have good health do not realise how blessed they are.

23. A man isn't truly respected by the kind of money he has, but by the kind of value he offers and the class he exhibits.

24. Sometimes, your environment determines your appearance.

25. Three kinds of people you should never underestimate are an angry man, a man in love, and a purpose-driven man, because they can do anything.

26. It's okay to lose at times; sometimes, losing gives you the experience and knowledge to win bigger things.

27. I don't believe you should play foolish to catch the wise; a wise man knows you're trying to get to him.

28. Sometimes, feeling scared is a good feeling. It makes us wiser.

29. Death can sometimes make you famous—more famous than you were when you were alive.

30. It is better to remain who you are than act hypocritically for human favour.

31. Those who give the best advice face the most problems. I'm living proof.

 32. That you're in the slums doesn't mean you're from the slums or should dress or act like someone from the slums.

33. If you can tolerate any kind of behaviour from people, then you'll go far in life.

34. A man who believes in his heart that he will become successful will keep trying no matter how many times he fails or how many years it takes.

35. Patience helps you listen to whatever people have to say, no matter how senseless they may sound or how meaningless their words are.

36. Practice makes perfect, but you need patience to practice.

35. A wolf hunts and thrives in its pack, but it wouldn't thrive so much if some were hunting for prey while others grazed.

36. A valuable man doesn't seek opportunity; it finds him.

37. The best way to make a good decision is to consider the advantages and disadvantages and to see things from different perspectives.

38. The first form of responsibility is taking responsibility for your actions.

39. Since mistakes are inevitable, why not learn from them?

40. If you think you're the best, endeavour to be better, and if you think you're the worst, endeavour to be better.

41. Everything I see people do inspire me to do the same thing or something entirely different.

42. Mistakes make you wiser because you learn not to repeat the same old things that didn't work or change certain things so the same old things can work.

43. Madness is simply seeing something from a different and abnormal perspective.

45. You're naive if you don't know what to do, but you're foolish if you know what to do but don't.

46. Ideas live longer on paper than in the brain.

47. We were never built to be impeccable, but we were built with the ability to improve.

48. We are not happy with what we have because we feel we deserve more.

49. The easiest way to be happy is to accept everything you have in good faith, but the most difficult way is to know you're built for more and work towards achieving more.

50. Everything you do has the potential to fail or succeed. It solely depends on how you implement it.

51. Persistence is a very powerful tool because the more you try to do something, the more you figure out how to do it properly.

52. Time isn't your friend; it's your servant. The good thing is that it can be a very good servant.

53. The first step in achieving anything is believing you can get it done.

54. We were never created to understand everything about life, but we were built with the ability to learn.

55. An ignorant man is like a man with a stiff neck; he can only see what's in front of him.

56. You will be a waste if you die unknown because the creator never built you to be mediocre.

57. Don't crawl if you were born to soar.

55. A woman who reads is dangerous, but a man who reads is powerful, and he should not be messed with.

56. Working out helps keep your body in shape, while meditating helps keep your mind in shape.

57. Humans are fragile creatures; they can be broken physically and emotionally.

58. A man can be a man and still not be a man.

59. If you tell yourself something often enough, your mind ingests it, and it becomes your truth.

60. To become a millionaire, you have to think, act, and talk like one. Then the millions start coming in.

61. Before something can grow, it must first be born. Start first and grow later.

62. What you do every day either brings you closer to achieving your goals or pushes you away from them.

63. Everything around us has the ability to make or break us.

64. A seed cannot maximise its potential if it is not buried in the soil.

65. There are certain kinds of people you will have around you, and some make failure difficult, while others make success a tedious task.

66. You need people to make money, even if you're an armed robber. Honour all men.

67. By hearing the bad and the good, you decide which you want to do.

68. You become more confident when you know what to do or say in every situation.

69. Unpredictability and discreetness are two weapons you can use to conquer your enemies.

70. Your location can affect your ability to save, invest, or earn.

71. A man cannot achieve anything if he doesn't have something pushing him to do so.

72. People only begin to care about the process when they see the results.

73. Most times, much is needed to achieve much.

74. Sometimes, how far you go isn't determined by the people you know but by how much you know.

75. You can actually change people without changing yourself.

76. Financial literacy is the first step to financial freedom.

77. To know and do what is good, one must first know what is bad.

78. Wealth comes to those who learn how to create it and implement wealth-creation methods.

79. To make money on a continent like Africa, you need something strong to push you.

80. What will be will be, but sometimes we have to make it or give it a slight push.

81. The beauty of integrity cannot be fully explained in words.

82. So many people fail in life as a result of misinformation that was forged out of bad listening skills.

83. It is possible to please everyone, but it is the most difficult task.

84. Most times, the fact that you know a wealthy person is more prestigious than being wealthy.

85. At times, people don't listen to you; they just observe you and how you sound. Always endeavour to sound classy.

86. If you want your children to be financially free, don't just send them to school; educate them on money and finance.

87. One man's source of pain is another man's paradise.

88. Fathers fight battles so their children can have peace.

89. Becoming successful in Africa is very difficult but not impossible, and it can be achieved when you have a strong push or source of motivation.

90. If you can recognise and satisfy a demand, you can make money.

91. When God wants to teach you a lesson, he uses people, and if you fail to learn, he uses circumstances.

92. People only begin to care about the process when they see the results.

93. Circumstances lead to certain events.

94. Something or someone can only begin to achieve or do more when they realise they were created for more.

95. No matter who we are, one day we will meet our ends. Make the most of your life.

96. Experience is the best teacher, and those who learn from experience are outstanding students.

97. Sometimes, you never get answers because you ask the wrong questions.

98. There comes a time in our lives where a dilemma kicks in and everything doesn't feel right, but it is left for us to fix ourselves.

99. If you can succeed once, then you'll keep succeeding, unless you're foolish. Success is only difficult the first time.

100. Mockery is usually initiated by people with no foresight or those with bad judgement skills.

101. To know the route you'll follow; you must first know where you are going.

102. Wealth creation is a slow process; you learn and you grow.

103. True greatness is characterised by how many lives you touch, how many people you help or influence, and how many souls you lift up.

104. The easiest way to make people like you is to agree with whatever they say. You become an enemy when you try to contradict them.

105. Striving for perfection is a complete waste of time because nothing can be completely perfect.

106. Approach each problem with the intention of solving it, and a solution will come forth.

107. It is very good to take risks, but it is much safer to take calculated risks.

108. When you are persistent enough, stubborn and resistant things lose their ability to remain stubborn and succumb to you.

109. Most times, people only begin to care about the process when they see the result.

110. If you succeed once, then you can keep succeeding; success is only difficult the first time.

111. Conversation enables connection, and connection facilitates sales.

EPILOGUE

Now you have learned how to rise above the limitations of age, colour, gender, and race. It's time to get working. A tree does not spring up unless a seed is buried in the soil. Knowledge becomes a waste if it is not utilized. Apply these lessons to your life, and you'll be unrecognisable in a short time. Whenever you think the odds are against you again, always remember that wealth doesn't belong only to a certain kind of person. It belongs to all; you just have to take your share.

Get up and start doing whatever will make your life better. Always remember that you were never born for mediocrity, and do your best to repel mediocrity. Walk in line with the wishes of your creator and seek to create value. Sacrifice anything that is good to get to wherever you want to get to. It doesn't matter how many times you fail; keep trying and keep pushing because one can never fail forever.

Rising above the limitations of age, colour, race, or even gender can be very difficult, but not impossible.

Sometimes, we have an incredible idea that we believe has the potential to be successful, but it is destroyed by society in its birthing stage.

I asked myself a very important question that changed my life: "How do people get rich in a poor country? Then I realised that a nation's poor economy has little to no effect on those who truly desire success. This is because if one thing doesn't work, another will. This book is packed with secrets backed up with quotes that will help you rise above the limitations placed on you by age, colour, race, or gender.

Rising above the barriers of age, colour, race, or even gender can be quite challenging, but it's important to remember that it is not impossible. Sometimes, we have incredible ideas that we believe can lead to success, but they face resistance from society in their early stages. At one point in my life, I asked myself a crucial question that completely transformed my journey: "How do people become wealthy in a poor country?" What I discovered is that a nation's economic challenges have little to no impact on those who are truly determined to achieve success. This is because if one approach doesn't work, there are always other paths to explore.

Throughout this book, I've shared valuable secrets and insights, supported by inspiring quotes, to help you break free from the limitations imposed on you by factors such as age, skin colour, race, or gender.

Each one of us carries immense potential within us, waiting to be unlocked. It doesn't matter where you come from or what challenges you face; your dreams are valid, and your ambitions can become a reality. The key is to persist in the face of adversity and to keep searching for solutions even when obstacles seem insurmountable. Success often requires resilience—the ability to bounce back from setbacks and keep moving forward. Remember that many famous individuals faced rejection, criticism, and adversity before achieving their goals. Their stories serve as a testament to the fact that, with determination and perseverance, you can overcome any obstacle.

Our world is a diverse tapestry of cultures, backgrounds, and talents. Don't see your unique qualities as obstacles; instead, embrace them as strengths. Different perspectives and experiences can be the driving force behind innovation and success. Throughout this book, you've encountered words of wisdom from individuals who have made their mark on the world. Let these quotes serve as beacons of inspiration as you navigate your own path to success.

As you close this book, remember that your journey is far from over. In fact, it's just beginning. The lessons and insights you've gained here are tools you can use to build a brighter future for yourself and those around you. No matter where you are on your path to success, keep moving forward, keep pushing boundaries, and keep believing in yourself.

The limitations of age, colour, race, or gender are challenges to be faced head-on, not barriers that can't be crossed. You have the power to shape your destiny, and the world is waiting to see what you can achieve. So, go forth with confidence, resilience, and the unwavering belief that you can rise above any limitations and reach the heights of success you've always dreamed of. Your journey is your own, and it is bound to be remarkable.

CONTACT US

Young Black Millionaire Africa (YBMA), is a platform that provides financial literacy, business education, inspiration, and motivation to those who feel their financial incapacitation is a result of the odds against them. Do you want to connect with us? You can reach us through the following mediums:

1. Email: youngblackmillionaire.mgt@gmail.com

2. Phone number: +2348142814580

3. Instagram: we_areybm

4. Twitter: YBM_Africa

5: Facebook: Young Black Millionaire

6. Tiktok: ybm_africa

7. YouTube: Young Black Millionaire Africa

 We are waiting to hear from you.

ABOUT THE AUTHOR

Ezedi Souvenir Isaac is a dynamic young entrepreneur, writer, blogger, tech enthusiast, and passionate advocate for cryptocurrencies. Hailing from Delta State, Nigeria, he is the youngest of four siblings, born on January 31st in the early 2000s.

Ezedi's entrepreneurial spirit ignited at a young age, and he had the unwavering support of his family from the start. As a child, he embarked on several business ventures, and many of them proved to be successful. Drawing from these early experiences, Ezedi Souvenir has distilled the invaluable secrets to success that he discovered into this book, with the sincere intention of sharing his knowledge and empowering others.

He is the visionary founder of "Young Black Millionaire Africa," a platform dedicated to providing financial literacy, business education, and inspiration to individuals who may have faced financial challenges or believe that certain odds are stacked against them. Ezedi Souvenir's journey and insights are a testament to the boundless potential within all of us. Through his work and this book, he aspires to uplift and bless others with the wisdom he has gained along his remarkable journey.